MALORIE BLACKMAN

Malorie Blackman has written over seventy books for children and young adults, including the *Noughts & Crosses* series, *Thief* and her science-fiction thriller *Chasing the Stars*. The fifth novel in her *Noughts & Crosses* sequence, *Crossfire*, was published by Penguin Random House Children's in 2019.

Malorie wrote for the eleventh series of *Doctor Who* starring Jodie Whittaker, co-writing the episode *Rosa* with Chris Chibnall, which was honoured at the inaugural Visionary Honours Awards 2019 for making 'a positive social impact'.

Her work has also been adapted for TV with the six-part adaptation of *Pig-Heart Boy* winning a BAFTA, and a major production of *Noughts + Crosses* launched by the BBC in 2020. *Noughts & Crosses* has been adapted for the stage by Dominic Cooke for the Royal Shakespeare Company, and by Sabrina Mahfouz for Pilot's 2019 UK tour.

In 2005, Malorie was honoured with the Eleanor Farjeon Award in recognition of her distinguished contribution to the world of children's books. In 2008 she received an OBE for her services to children's literature and, between 2013 and 2015, she was the Children's Laureate.

SABRINA MAHFOUZ

Sabrina Mahfouz is a writer and performer. Her most recent theatre show was *A History of Water in the Middle East* (Royal Court, 2019), which her forthcoming debut non-fiction book is inspired by, *These Bodies of Water* (Tinder Press, 2022).

Her most recent publications as editor include *Smashing It: Working Class Artists on Life, Art and Making it Happen* (Saqi, 2019) and *Poems From a Green and Blue Planet* (Hachette, 2019). She is a resident writer at Shakespeare's Globe Theatre and at the TV and film company, House Productions.

NOUGHTS & CROSSES

based on the novel
by Malorie Blackman

adapted by Sabrina Mahfouz

NICK HERN BOOKS

London

www.nickhernbooks.co.uk

A Nick Hern Book

This stage adaptation of *Noughts & Crosses* first published as a paperback original in Great Britain in 2020 by Nick Hern Books Limited, The Glasshouse, 49a Goldhawk Road, London W12 8QP

Stage adaptation of *Noughts & Crosses* copyright © 2020 Sabrina Mahfouz

Noughts & Crosses copyright © 2001 Oneta Malorie Blackman
First published in Great Britain by Doubleday 2001, Corgi edition published 2002

Sabrina Mahfouz has asserted her right to be identified as the author of this adaptation

Cover image: Heather Agyepong (Sephy) and Billy Harris (Callum) in the original production of *Noughts & Crosses*, 2019; photograph by Robert Day

Designed and typeset by Nick Hern Books, London
Printed in Great Britain by CPI Group (Ltd), Croydon CR0 4YY

ISBN 978 1 84842 923 9

A CIP catalogue record for this book is available from the British Library

Introduction

Sabrina Mahfouz, adapter

Noughts & Crosses is a book which leaps from the page into every reader's heart. It is a book Malorie Blackman was 'advised' not to write. Thank the skies she did it anyway! And here we are, over twenty years later, with a new theatre adaptation and a television series of the story.

Working my way meticulously through the book, it was startlingly easy to see why it continues to grow into new mediums – it is sadly far too close to our reality to leave our imaginations. We still live in a systemically racist society, no matter how loudly this may be refuted by those at the top of it. Opportunities are still largely determined by what background you are born into, no matter how many like to, or need to, believe that we live in a meritocracy.

The racism within Britain must be addressed in every area of life, not deflected as just an 'American/historical/colonial' thing. *Noughts & Crosses* does not allow deflection, even as it's set in an anonymous location at an unspecified time. Due to the intensity of Sephy and Callum's individual journeys, Malorie makes their world ours. This is what I wanted to draw out on stage the most. These two flawed, fantastic, brave, young people – in love, lost, full of hope and rage, dreams and desires, challenging a supremacist system just by being their complicated selves.

It was a huge honour to adapt such an epic, important, adored book, and it was only made possible with the dedicated hard work of all at Pilot Theatre and all of the astounding actors and members of the original creative team.

Esther Richardson, director

We began working on *Noughts & Crosses* at Pilot in December 2016, when I first had the honour to meet Malorie Blackman.

This book means so much to so many, though I've never forgotten Malorie telling me that her greatest wish was for *Noughts & Crosses* to no longer be so relevant. The summer before we met, an MP, Jo Cox, had been murdered by a far-right activist, and the EU referendum result had led to sharp rises in racist and xenophobic attacks across the UK. Staging this piece of work felt necessary and urgent at the end of 2016, and that feeling has only intensified.

What Malorie presents in this story could first appear to be a more extreme context with its racial segregation, capital punishment and systemic oppression of a single community, but we neither need look very far into our own difficult history as a country, nor survey the communities we live in especially deeply, to see the sharpest of truths and parallels with here and now.

When you read this script, what you won't see are the processes that have led us to this presentation of the story. Race, gender, class, mental health and identity are just some of the huge subjects we've interrogated as a company, as fearlessly as possible. It's been vital to have a fully open casting process, and a creative team who were able to bring their own lived experiences of these subjects into the rehearsal room to inform our work. It's also been vital to develop the piece in parallel with work with young people, inviting a group of them to be part of the process.

Making *Noughts & Crosses* has been a huge journey and a special collaboration. My sincere thanks to everyone who has supported its translation to the stage. There is a great deal of division in the world at the moment, but there are still the radical, powerful forces of kindness, empathy, compassion and love. The whole project has made us not only interrogate, respect and seek to understand our differences, but also brought us together in solidarity in the space of theatre, to learn again what connects us and what we are prepared to fight for: a world where we can truly be equals, and where we can love whom we choose.

This adaptation of Malorie Blackman's *Noughts & Crosses* by Sabrina Mahfouz was commissioned and first produced by Pilot Theatre in a co-production with Derby Theatre, Belgrade Theatre Coventry, Mercury Theatre Colchester and York Theatre Royal. It was first performed at Derby Theatre on 1 February 2019, before touring the UK.

The cast was as follows (in alphabetical order):

SEPHY	Heather Agyepong
JASMINE	Doreene Blackstock
JUDE	Jack Condon
RYAN	Daniel Copeland
CALLUM	Billy Harris
MEGGIE	Lisa Howard
KAMAL	Chris Jack
MINERVA	Kimisha Lewis

All other roles played by the company, as detailed in the suggested doubling.

Director	Esther Richardson
Designer	Simon Kenny
Lighting Designer	Joshua Drualus Pharo
Associate Director/Movement	Corey Campbell
Music and Sound	Arun Ghosh and Xana
Video Designer	Ian William Galloway
Fight Director	Kenan Ali
Production Sound Engineer	Adam McCready
Associate Video Designer	Rafael Vartanian
Production Manager (*Derby*)	Andy Nairn
Production Manager (*Tour*)	Andy Reader
Company Stage Manager	Sarah Rhodes Cannings
Assistant Stage Manager	Lizzie Rodipe

Technical Stage Manager	Paul Williams
Tour Set Manager	Luke James
Relighter	Paul Salmon
Creative Associates	Catherine Palmer and Oliver O'Shea
National Press and PR	Duncan Clarke PR
Production Photographs	Robert Day
Production Trailers	Fresh Label
Production Departments	Derby Theatre
Set Construction	Belgrade Theatre Coventry

Special thanks to Suzann McLean, Young & Talented Theatre, and all the Noughts & Crosses *Young Creatives.*

FOR PILOT THEATRE

Artistic Director	Esther Richardson
Executive Producer	Amanda J Smith
Company Administrator	Sarah Rorke
Marketing & Projects Producer	Lucy Hammond
Digital Officer	Sam Johnson

pilot-theatre.com
@pilot_theatre

NOUGHTS & CROSSES

Malorie Blackman

adapted for the stage by
Sabrina Mahfouz

2

Characters

SEPHY HADLEY, *Black/Cross young woman, aged thirteen to eighteen*

CALLUM McGREGOR, *White/Nought young man, aged fifteen to twenty*

THE HADLEYS (Crosses)
JASMINE, *Mum*
KAMAL, *Dad, the Home Secretary*
MINERVA, *Sephy's sister*

THE McGREGORS (Noughts)
MEGGIE, *Mum*
RYAN, *Dad*
JUDE, *Callum's brother*
LYNETTE, *Callum's sister*

ANDREW, *a member of the Liberation Militia*
SHANIA, *a Nought schoolgirl*
MR BOWDEN, *a teacher at Heathcroft School*
LOLA, *a Cross schoolgirl*
DIONNE, *a Cross schoolgirl*
KELANI ADAMS QC, *a Cross lawyer*
MR PINGULE, *a Cross lawyer*
JUDGE ANDERSON
MORGAN, *a member of the Liberation Militia*
JACKIE, *a Cross prison guard*
EXECUTIONER
PRISON GOVERNOR
PRISON OFFICER

Plus PROTESTORS, SCHOOLCHILDREN, POLICE, REPORTERS, LIBERATION MILITIA MEMBERS, GUARDS

Suggested Doubling for Eight Actors

ACTOR 1 – Sephy

ACTOR 2 – Callum

ACTOR 3 – Jude / Protestor / Nought Schoolboy

ACTOR 4 – Ryan / Andrew / Protestor

ACTOR 5 – Meggie / Lynette / Shania / Morgan

ACTOR 6 – Jasmine / Protestor / Dionne / Judge / Jackie

ACTOR 7 – Minerva / Protestor / Lola / Kelani Adams

ACTOR 8 – Kamal / Protestor / Mr Bowden / Policeman /
          Mr Pingule

Note on Stage Directions and Scenes

Stage directions are purposefully sparse, to enable the
producing company to represent this complicated world in the
way that best uses the physical space and vision that they have.

Similarly, scenes are not formally named or numbered to
encourage as much seamless flowing into each other as
possible, to keep the pace fast and tense. There are gaps to show
when 'a change' of location has occurred, but this is to be
interpreted by the company at their discretion.

A forward slash (/) indicates where the next speaking character
interrupts.

Prologue

A baby is crying. The ensemble enter.

Grown-up SEPHY HADLEY *and* CALLUM McGREGOR
watch as –

MEGGIE McGREGOR *picks up Sephy from her cradle to
console her.*

Two-year-old Callum sleeps nearby.

JASMINE HADLEY *appears in the room – she watches*
MEGGIE *for a beat.*

ENSEMBLE. When a newborn baby cries
   it means there's life
   and with new life there's new hope,
   right?

MEGGIE. She's perfect, Mrs Hadley. Persephone, such a pretty
   name.

JASMINE. Thank you, Meggie. I'm sure her and your Callum
   will be… great friends.

MEGGIE. He'll be the luckiest boy in the world if they are,
   Mrs Hadley.

   MEGGIE *passes Sephy to* JASMINE, *deferentially but
   lovingly.*

SEPHY. And we *were* friends. Best friends.

CALLUM. And I *was* the luckiest boy in the world.

CALLUM/SEPHY. I remember –

SEPHY. Leapfrogging over rocks, sleeping in trees –

CALLUM. Sneaking in and out of sand-dune dens –

SEPHY. Toes tickled by the cold sea
   even though we weren't supposed to be by the water –

CALLUM. Not supposed to be anywhere we couldn't be seen,
   but we were always –

SEPHY. Hiding –

CALLUM. Smiling –

SEPHY. Climbing –

CALLUM. Laughing…

   Beat.

SEPHY. Then –

   And the scene suddenly shifts.

   CALLUM *and* SEPHY *are kids running around* JASMINE
   and MEGGIE.

   But the two women are still and tense.

   Something has obviously just been said that has shocked
   MEGGIE.

   KAMAL HADLEY *enters.*

KAMAL. Is it true?
   Is it true?
   Has my wife been here with you?
   Are you not my housekeeper? Will you not answer me?
   Must I roar even more, even louder?

JASMINE. Meggie, just tell Mr Hadley – tell him
   we were in the house with the children all last night.

   Beat.

KAMAL. Meggie, you will speak.

   Beat.

MEGGIE. Mr Hadley, I respect you as my boss
   and your wife,
   dare I say it, as my friend.

Even so, sir,
us Noughts have to find dignity where we can
and… I find it in truth.

KAMAL. So what is it then, your dignifying truth?

Beat.

MEGGIE. Sorry, Mrs Hadley –

JASMINE. Get out, get out, get out!

KAMAL *roars, the* KIDS *run away and we are left with*
JASMINE *and* MEGGIE *on their own on opposite sides of
the stage.* CALLUM *and* SEPHY *begin their new reality –*

CALLUM. We didn't understand what had happened.

SEPHY. But we knew our games had to change now.

CALLUM. No more playing in Sephy's family grounds,
as we wondered if our mums would ever speak again.

SEPHY. *We* were still speaking, they couldn't stop us, nobody
could –
we were partners in crime. Two of a kind.

CALLUM. Biding our time, till we had an excuse to be together
in the open every day.

SEPHY. For three years we only ever met in secret – on my
family's private beach, which I can see now is so crazy, to
have our own beach, but at the time, it was just our place,
mine and Callum's, with the ocean in front of us and the
wide world waiting for us…

ACT ONE

SEPHY *and* CALLUM *sit on the beach.* CALLUM *is muttering to himself with a calculator in his hands, working out sums.* SEPHY *has a sketchbook and a pencil out, but feels ignored.*

SEPHY. I command the sea never to move again!
    I clap my hands and there is fire in my palms!
    I use the fire to… draw.
    To draw you. Your amazing hair.

    SEPHY *draws.*

    Look! Look? Callum? Callum.

CALLUM. Not even *you* can command the sea to stop moving, Sephy.

SEPHY. So I shouldn't even try?

CALLUM. What you should do, is your maths homework, you've had all summer to do it. And my hair isn't amazing. It's just my hair.

SEPHY. When did you get so serious and boring?

CALLUM. When I turned fifteen. And found out I'll be at Heathcroft School in a class with kids two years younger than me.

SEPHY. Hey, I'm going to be in your class and I'm fourteen next month!

CALLUM. Exactly – kids!

SEPHY. Only a year and a bit younger than you, so stop with the patronising, pleeease.

CALLUM. Sorry. It's just, history is being made tomorrow – Noughts going to a Cross school. To your school.

SEPHY. Like we've wanted for eternity! Aren't you excited?

CALLUM. For maths.

SEPHY. Ugh. I'd skip every maths class for the rest of time if I could.

CALLUM. Draw your way through life?

SEPHY. Why not? Makes way more sense than counting your way through.

CALLUM. Guess it depends.

SEPHY. On what?

CALLUM. On whether you can afford to be wrong. The first mathematician was a Nought – did you know that?

SEPHY. No.

CALLUM *smiles*.

CALLUM. Cos they only tell you about Noughts doing 'big bad stuff'.

SEPHY. Tell the teachers that tomorrow!

CALLUM. Oh yeah, get myself expelled on my first day, like an 'ungrateful Nought'. Nah, I'll just cross out all the lies in the history books one by one over the next three years till it's one big sea of Biro and they have to rewrite them!

They laugh.

Maybe I should call them out. They might kick me out after a day no matter what I do anyway.

SEPHY. No they won't!

Beat.

Callum, think of all the Nought kids who went for that scholarship. They really are trying to open up and I think you'll be surprised, a lot of Crosses are excited about this, you're going to smash it tomorrow.

CALLUM. Maybe…

SEPHY. And just think, we can do normal stuff – have lunch together, chat by the lockers, sit side by side.

CALLUM. Yeah.

SEPHY. Do you want to see my drawing?

CALLUM. Of my amazing hair?

SEPHY. And your fascinating forehead.

CALLUM. Only if you'll take a look at these equations.

SEPHY*'s phone goes.*

SEPHY. Ha, saved from maths by Mother! She can be useful every now and again. (*Reading.*) Oh, she's flipping out – I better go.

CALLUM. Tomorrow: schools for Noughts… The future: we might even be allowed mobile phones too!

SEPHY. It's fun the way we do it though. Waiting at my window for your whistle. Like a film.

CALLUM. A film?! You do make me laugh, Sephy.

SEPHY. Can I ask you something?

CALLUM. Sure.

SEPHY….Can I kiss you?

CALLUM. What? Why?

SEPHY. Um. I just thought. Well, I don't want to get to fourteen and not have kissed anyone and you're my best friend and I trust you and I tell you everything even all the stuff about my mum basically being an alcoholic and –

During this, CALLUM *presents his face for* SEPHY *to kiss it and she pulls back. He's embarrassed. Then she goes to kiss him too but before their lips meet –*

Another text message interrupts them.

They awkwardly smile, laugh. SEPHY *reads the message and rolls her eyes.*

Mum again.

CALLUM. Go on then. I'll see you – and the drawing –
    tomorrow.
    At school.

SEPHY. Callum?

CALLUM. Yeah?

SEPHY. You passed that exam and it proved you're exceptional
    and you deserve to be at Heathcroft, okay!?

CALLUM. I know you mean well, yeah, but no Nought should
    have to be exceptional to get the same as average Crosses
    though, should they, Sephy?

SEPHY. Hey, who you calling average?…

*They need to say goodbye. This is the moment. They kiss. It
is very short and sweet and tender and then they break off
and both run home.*

MINERVA HADLEY, SEPHY*'s sister, and* JUDE
McGREGOR, CALLUM*'s brother, are watching television in
their respective houses.*

REPORTER. Liberation Members found guilty for the car
    bomb outside the International Trade Centre last month have
    been issued the death sentence today. Home Secretary,
    Kamal Hadley, issued this statement earlier –

MINERVA. Dad's on telly, Mum!

JASMINE *enters, holding glass of wine, to watch* –

KAMAL. Political terrorism which results in the death or injury
    of even just one Cross always has been and always will be a
    capital crime. It is right that those found guilty suffer the
    death sentence –

JUDE *switches over to a different channel.*

JUDE. Blah blah blah!

REPORTER. Protests both for and against the Nought children due to start at Cross schools tomorrow have continued outside Parliament tonight, with fears of violence between opposing sides –

MEGGIE. Give us a break for God's sake, even better, give us our own decent schools so we can stay well clear of yours!

SEPHY, MINERVA *and* JASMINE *sit around the table with mobile phones.*

SEPHY. Minnie, can you pass the orange juice?

MINERVA. How many times do I have to tell you not to call me Minnie? My name is Minerva. M. I. N. E. R. V. A.

SEPHY. Yes. Minnie.

JASMINE. Minerva. Pass Sephy the orange juice.

SEPHY. Are you eating later again, Mother?

JASMINE (*gulping wine*). Yes.

SEPHY. I love the night before the first day back at school, it's so –

MINERVA. Don't talk about it.

SEPHY. Why not?

MINERVA. Who ever wants to be reminded of going back to Heathcroft? Let alone when three actual Noughts are going to be starting. Urgh.

SEPHY. What do you mean 'urgh'? What have they ever done to you?

MINERVA. What have they ever done *for* you?

JASMINE. Girls, please, my head.

SEPHY. It's Dad's policy, though, he says it's a 'slow and steady / first step' –

MINERVA. ' – first step', yes, Sephy, we've all heard him on telly. Because that's the only place we *ever* hear him –

JASMINE. Can we just have a nice, quiet dinner –

MINERVA. Don't you have an opinion on it, Mother? On Noughts coming to our schools – to mine and Sephy's school, even?

JASMINE. Your father believes it is the right thing to do –

MINERVA. Or he just had to do *something* to stop the Pangean Economic Community sanctions against us?

SEPHY. No, it's cos it's time, Dad wouldn't be so –

MINERVA. Politician-like? Strategic? Come on, Sephy, nearly every other Pangean country gives Noughts passports now, we're considered regressive –

SEPHY. Why are you against things changing then?

MINERVA. I just don't see any good coming of it, but we'll find out tomorrow I suppose.

The women focus on their mobiles as we switch to –

RYAN. Whether they like it or not, lad, you'll be at a Cross school tomorrow! Imagine that.

MEGGIE. I still think it's a big mistake.

RYAN. Well I don't.

MEGGIE. We don't need to mix with them.

JUDE. Haven't we even got a bit of milk?

RYAN. You know we can only get milk on Fridays now, Jude.

JUDE. I'm *so sick* of water water water.

RYAN. Oi! How about a bit of gratitude for once?

CALLUM. Why would you say that, what's wrong with mixing, Mum?

MEGGIE. It doesn't work. As long as Crosses run the schools –
and everything else – we'll always be second-class nothings.
We should educate our own. Teach our kids about the
Noughts who've made a difference in this world – instead of
letting them disappear out of history. Make them see they
can be more than the Crosses will let them think they can be.

RYAN. You never used to believe that.

MEGGIE. I'm not as naive as I used to be.

RYAN. Meggie, if our boy is going to get anywhere in this life,
if he's not going to wind up working at the dump, the
lumberyard, cleaning up after Crosses –

JUDE. It's not easy to get those jobs either, you know –

RYAN. – he has to go to their schools. He has to learn to play
the game. He just has to be better at it, that's all.

MEGGIE. That's all?

RYAN. Don't you want something better for him than we've
had?

MEGGIE. Ryan, how can you even question that!?

CALLUM. Stop –

JUDE. And what about better than what I've had? Can't even
get an apprenticeship and you just care about Callum. Best
thing about tomorrow is Callum'll finally find out he's not as
special as you two make out –

MEGGIE. That's enough, Jude!

RYAN. You should be happy for your brother, you know, that he
has this opportunity, that things are finally changing!

MINERVA. May I sleepover at Hermione's on Saturday?

JASMINE *gulps down what is left of a glass of wine.*

JASMINE. Do whatever you want, as long as it brings no
shame to the Hadley family name.

MINERVA. As if the name isn't shamed enough already.

JASMINE. Minerva, if you have a problem with your father's policies, you can speak to him about –

MINERVA. If he was ever here, then I would –

JASMINE. Minerva!

MINERVA *goes*.

SEPHY. Well, I'm excited for tomorrow, I'm going to welcome the Noughts no matter what.

JASMINE. Persephone, when I say no shame is to be brought to this name, this house, I mean that, do you understand?

SEPHY. Yes, Mother.
(*Under her breath*.) It's as crystal clear as the bottom of your glass.

RYAN. You just go there tomorrow and hold your head up high, son, show those Crosses that we Noughts respect ourselves and won't be intimidated or –

CALLUM. Or I might just go there to learn, Dad, cos that's why I'm going. Not to be the rent-a-Nought for Crosses with a conscience –

JUDE. No such thing –

CALLUM. They're not all bad, Jude.

JUDE. What, you mean your little Cross girlfriend? That Sephy Hadley? She's a – bitch!

RYAN. Jude!

JUDE. What? Cos of that family we've been at the bottom of the / pile for years now –

MEGGIE. It was just cos I didn't lie about Jasmine, / I –

RYAN. Jude! What is / with you?

MEGGIE. I don't like to lie, why / should I lie?

JUDE. Nothing is 'with' me, Dad, I just get pissed off that the
Hadleys messed up our lives and Callum still chases after
that Sephy, sipping secret orange juice or whatever they –

RYAN. You've had orange juice!

CALLUM *is fuming, silently.*

JUDE. You fancy her, don't you? You think one day you two
will – what? What do you think? You gonna make babies
that won't know what or who they are? You're as mad as
Lynette!

MEGGIE/RYAN. Jude!

CALLUM *has stood up and wants to hit* JUDE, *but walks
away instead.*

MEGGIE. Callum! You haven't finished!

JUDE *has stormed off in the opposite direction.*

Jude!

MEGGIE *goes after* CALLUM *and indicates for* RYAN *to
go after* JUDE.

Only SEPHY *and* JASMINE *are left at the long table.*

SEPHY. Three years.
Three years since I've seen the regal Mrs Hadley sober.
How can I bring shame to a drunkard mother
in a silent house?
And I hate to say it but Minnie's right –
a father more taken with Parliament
than partaking in family arguments
or even, imagine, family daytrips
or how about dinner once a week?
Forget it, just drink more wine.
It must be truly terrible to live a life
you thought you never would.
But you shouldn't hide away, you should face things,
make decisions.

JASMINE, *noticing her wine glass is empty, exits.*

I promise myself I will.
My life will be better, it will be bolder
and it will be braver than all of yours.

CALLUM. Three years.
Three years since – they labelled my big sister as mad.
Three years since Mum got fired
and my house's default decor has been *sad*.
The paint peels. The floors creak. The sofa sinks.
Nobody thinks. It's just chit-chat or shouting,
no inbetween, no 'how have you really been?'
Three years since Lynette's come down the stairs.

Light up on LYNETTE.

She's just stuck up there in her room, heard but never seen.
When she looks in the mirror she sees a Cross, would you
believe?
Mum and Dad have taken her for help, for relief
of all the pain she's clearly in – but *they* say
'No, sorry, we can't help with mental illness',
Like to them it's not real –
cos a wasted Nought's life's no big deal...
Three years it's been now – how it used to be?
I don't even know.
But tomorrow: *tomorrow* –
Heathcroft School is my school.
And no matter what *they* say, tomorrow,
I'm gonna make my way to the life I really want.

KAMAL *leads a Nought man,* ANDREW, *into the dining room.*

Simultaneously, as we hear KAMAL *talking,* SEPHY *is in her
bedroom and has got everything ready for school in the
morning. She is about to go to sleep. She needs a drink. She
wanders to the dining room.*

KAMAL. Those bleeding-heart Liberals in the Pangean Economic Community make me sick! Haven't I done enough? 'Give Noughts places in the police and army,' they said – and I did. 'Give Noughts places in the schools,' and well, well – I've done that too. And they're *still* not satisfied. As for the Liberation Militia –

ANDREW. Sir, a few school places won't appease a militant group like the Liberation Militia. They want a complete change of the system. A power shift.

KAMAL. That *is* why I'm paying *you* to infiltrate, inform and stop these terrorists – and their so-called pacifist allies.

SEPHY *hears* KAMAL*'s voice and is excited, so starts to run towards him.*

ANDREW. The Militia won't stop.

SEPHY *stops suddenly, hearing the other voice.*

They've had a few sweets from the bowl, now they want more.

SEPHY *sneaks in to listen.*

KAMAL. The sheer ingratitude! I knew this was a mistake.

ANDREW. They want –

KAMAL. Just who are 'they' anyway? Who's their leader?

ANDREW. Sir, I'm working on it. They are very careful, and they work in units –

SEPHY *makes a noise.* KAMAL *sees her.*

KAMAL. Sephy. Go to bed – NOW!

ANDREW *leaves abruptly.*

SEPHY *turns to rush off and* KAMAL *gets up to follow her.*

Princess – wait. I'm sorry for shouting. It's been a – long day.

SEPHY. That's okay.

KAMAL. Gosh, you've grown.

SEPHY. Probably I have, in the month since I've seen you.

KAMAL. You know how my work is, sweetheart. I'm sorry we never got to have our summer day out together. Soon, I'll take a day off, okay?

SEPHY *nods*.

Princess… What did you hear just then?

SEPHY. Nothing. I just came down for a drink and when I heard your voice, I was coming to say hello.

KAMAL. It was work stuff, private.

SEPHY. I didn't hear anything, just your voice, Dad.

KAMAL. Still my princess?

SEPHY *nods*. *They hug*.

Off to bed then.

SEPHY *makes her way to her room, as* KAMAL *makes a call to finish the conversation*.

We can't meet in person again, it's too risky. Message me as soon as you find out who the LM leader is. I'm not losing my place in this Government because of some terrorist rabble-rousers.

Blankers going to my daughter's school, it has to be enough. You tell them that. As I tell myself every night – God spare us from Liberals and bloody Blankers!

The kitchen is dark. SEPHY *is alone*.

SEPHY. Feet like ice, hands like fire.
The middle of me, maybe a glacier.
Something scary, moving slowly.
Finding its way to every bit of my body.
My father, the Home Secretary, Kamal Hadley –
Daddy.
He said it twice!
The 'B'-word.
B–L–A–N–K–E– I can't even spell it out.

I've never, ever heard it out loud before.
Only read it in books about when Noughts were made slaves.
I'm pretty sure the man he was speaking to
was a Nought himself –
how could he listen while my dad said that!?
Callum was right, nothing's actually simple,
it's all tainted, all complicated – more so than I ever thought.
He already knew that, maybe it's impossible not to,
as a Nought.

A group of PROTESTORS *outside the school.*

PROTESTORS. No no no to Noughts in our schools,
GO GO GO back to your own!
No no no to Noughts in our schools
GO GO GO back to your own!

CALLUM *is trying to get into the school past the*
PROTESTORS – *there's intimidating behaviour.* CALLUM
is desperately trying to get to SEPHY, *who is attempting,*
quite delicately, to get to him too.

The protest escalates to a point where a Nought girl,
SHANIA, *is hit by something.*

SEPHY. Stop it!
Let the Noughts pass!
Let Callum past! This is their school now too!

PROTESTOR. Traitor!

SEPHY *starts to be filmed?*

SEPHY. Stop it, let him through!

Nobody listens.

STOP!

Nobody listens, CALLUM *is being physically blocked from*
entering school. SEPHY *is completely invisible, she makes*
her biggest physical attempt to break the obstruction,
shouting as she does –

You're behaving like BLANKERS!

Silence. CALLUM *recoils.*

At the McGREGORS'.

RYAN. I went down to Heathcroft as soon as I heard but the police wouldn't let me in.

JUDE. Why not?

RYAN. I had no official business on the premises – unquote.

JUDE. Those bastards.

MEGGIE. Jude! As long as you're okay, Callum, love?

CALLUM. I'm okay. It's fine. We knew it wasn't going to be an easy ride. Once we got into school it was all right though.

JUDE. But your little girlfriend wasn't all right though, was she, filth that came out her mouth.

CALLUM. What?

JUDE. You think we wouldn't see all that on TV? Everyone saw it. Apple doesn't fall far from the tree and all that.

RYAN. Jude… Callum, perhaps best to try and stay away from her. I'll come with you tomorrow.

CALLUM. Dad, no –

JUDE. You're seriously going to let him go back? After what happened this morning?

RYAN. No Daggers are / going to –

CALLUM. Dad, don't call them that, please.

RYAN. No *Crosses* are going to drive my son from *his* school. His chance. Understand?

CALLUM. Yes, Dad.

Later at the beach, SEPHY *and* CALLUM *sit together, but apart.*

SEPHY. Sorry sorry sorry sorry sorry sorry sorry sorry –

CALLUM. Sephy. I know you are. But that word. Your mouth.

SEPHY. I… I've never said it before.

CALLUM. It wasn't just the word. It was what you meant.

SEPHY. What do you mean?

CALLUM. What did you mean? 'Behaving like – ' What do *we* behave like?

SEPHY. No. I meant, you know, how they try to make out Noughts behave, not how I think… I just wanted them to stop. I just wanted you to be safe.

CALLUM. You don't need to protect me.

SEPHY. Sorry. Again. So… Are we / all right –

CALLUM. I think… Sephy, it's best if, at school, we just keep away from each other. We can still meet here.

SEPHY. Oh.

CALLUM. The beach can still be ours, Sephy.

SEPHY. Okay. Yeah. Fine. If that's what you want.

CALLUM. It'll be easier that way, that's all.

SEPHY. I said fine.

CALLUM. Fine.

Beat.

SEPHY. No, actually.

CALLUM. No, what?

SEPHY. Why should we take the easy way out, who is it really easier for?

CALLUM. For me, obviously.

SEPHY. You're my… friend, my oldest friend. Why shouldn't we be friends at *our* school?

CALLUM. You saw why today.

SEPHY. I said sorry, a million times.

CALLUM. I'm not even talking about that. Not all of it is about you, Sephy, you're gonna have to grow up sooner or later and realise that. Look at the world around you – it's not all orange juice and sketchbooks.

Pause.

SEPHY. If that's what you think of me. It really is fine. We don't need to be friends at school, or anywhere, in fact. Because you know what, it's not all about you either.

SEPHY *runs off*.

At the McGREGORS'.

MEGGIE (*to the television*). Oh, here we go.

REPORTER. Today Kamal Hadley declared there would be no hiding place, no safe haven for those Noughts misguided enough to join the Liberation Militia, as a policy of tougher sentencing and extra funding for the counter-terrorism department was announced.

MEGGIE (*to the television*). What about an apology for what happened at Heathcroft, eh?

JUDE. They haven't shown that clip of Sephy since this morning.

RYAN. Kamal Hadley has changed up the agenda, hasn't he, all about the LM now, deflect the attention from the way Noughts are treated once again –

INTERVIEWER. Mr Hadley, these announcements will no doubt be very welcome to most law-abiding citizens, but isn't it true that the Liberation Militia *is* directly influencing Government decisions – the recent one to allow Noughts into Cross schools being a prime example?

KAMAL. No, no. This was about working on a Pangean Economic Community Directive. We are not going to be blackmailed by an illegal terrorist group.

JUDE (*standing and punching the air with a tight fist*). Course it was them! Long live the Liberation Militia!

MEGGIE. Jude!

RYAN. Meggie, you said it first – we'll never get anywhere as long as the Crosses run everything.

JUDE. The LM is the only way, Mum.

MEGGIE. You want to end up on death row? Violence gets us nowhere. And we're better than that. Don't need to stoop to his – (*Indicating* KAMAL.) level.

She switches the television off.

JUDE. Mum!

RYAN (*for* MEGGIE'*s benefit*). She's right, son. We're better than them.

MEGGIE. I'm going to take Lynny her dinner up.

   MEGGIE *leaves*.

CALLUM (*to* JUDE). You can't be serious?

RYAN. We're in serious times, son – someone has to stick up for us, don't they?

It is lunchtime in the school canteen. CALLUM *is on a table with other Noughts.*

SEPHY. Oh hi, Callum, can I sit here?

CALLUM. Um. I thought we –

   SEPHY *sits with her lunch tray. She smiles at the others, they look down.*

SEPHY. Hello, welcome to Heathcroft, everyone. I know yesterday was a bit of a nightmare but most people here are actually all right. I'm Sephy by the way, Sephy Hadley and –

NOUGHT BOY. We know who you are.

SEPHY. Oh. Listen, that word –

CALLUM. Sephy –

SEPHY. Is a terrible terrible word and I will regret saying it for the rest of my life. I'd like a chance to prove to you I'm not a *complete* ignorant idiot.

   CALLUM *can't help but smile at 'ignorant idiot'.*

NOUGHT BOY. Sorry, I'm not taking any chances. See you lot later.

   He leaves. SEPHY *is shocked but recovers composure.* SHANIA *takes the lead.*

SHANIA. My name's Shania.

   SHANIA *and* SEPHY *shake hands.*

SEPHY. So pleased to meet you, Shania. Sorry your face got cut.

SHANIA. I'm just sorry they don't sell plasters in my skin tone, to be honest! The cut itself, well, mark of what I'll fight for, I guess.

   MR BOWDEN *comes out from the Cross ensemble.*

MR BOWDEN. Persephone Hadley, what do you think you're doing?

SEPHY. Eating lunch, sir.

MR BOWDEN. Get to your own table, now.

SEPHY. Why can't I sit with my friends –

MR BOWDEN (*to* SHANIA). Are you friends with this girl?

SHANIA. No, sir.

MR BOWDEN. And you – Callum, isn't it? Are you friends with her?

   Pause.

CALLUM. No, sir, no… I'm not.

SEPHY *stands in horror as* MR BOWDEN *picks her up and drags her away.*

MR BOWDEN. They can never be your friends, Persephone, now move.

SHANIA. Good. She's fake as anything.

CALLUM. She… she just wants to do the right thing.

SHANIA. Ha! Come over like she's some kind of ambassador for peace? She just wants to feel special for sticking up for the underdog, then go back to her cosy little life of luxury and forget about us. As if we don't know who her dad is. He despises us. Would suffocate us with his own hands if he could get away with it!

CALLUM *is having an anxiety attack.*

CALLUM. It's like I hear crashing all around me.
    Waves or bricks or bits of wood, I dunno.
    It's just chaos and destruction
    and I'm walking right through the middle of it.
    I know something has to land on me eventually
    but till it does I'm finding it hard to –
    breathe.

SEPHY *has been moved to an area of the canteen, but people move away from wherever she is, like a reverse magnet.*

SEPHY. It's like I see the whole world I knew
    crashing all around me – was it ever real?
    I don't know.
    But one thing I do know
    for the first time in my life,
    I'm completely alone.

DIONNE *and* LOLA *begin their pursuit of* SEPHY.

The following happens simultaneously. The spoken dialogue between JUDE *and* CALLUM *occurs in its own time, whilst the corresponding scene is still physically 'live'. Underlining indicates lines/words that should be spoken simultaneously as far as possible.*

SEPHY *is moving slowly away from the canteen –*

She goes into a toilet cubicle and locks the door, crying.

DIONNE *and* LOLA *follow after her and discuss together briefly, then wait outside the cubicle door.*

JUDE. What you doing home at this time?

CALLUM. Just… wasn't feeling well.

JUDE. You look all right to me.

CALLUM. –

JUDE. Oh, lovely, the silent treatment, like that nutter upstairs.

CALLUM. Don't call her that –

JUDE. What other word is there? She's found her tongue this morning. Going on and on about being a bloody Dagger –

Eventually, SEPHY *dries her eyes and takes a deep breath, opens the door and gasps as she sees –*

CALLUM. Don't use that word. How hard is it to just say <u>Crosses</u> –

LOLA. <u>CROSSES</u>, Sephy. We are Crosses and we don't mix with *Blankers*. If you sit with them again, you'll find life very difficult.

SEPHY. <u>Why do you hate them so much?</u>

JUDE. <u>Why do you love them so much?</u>

LOLA. Don't you watch the news? They hate us.

SEPHY. No <u>they don't</u>. And the news lies, it's not the truth –

DIONNE. You are such a Blanker lover!

LOLA (*pushing her*). Yeah, <u>who do you think you are?</u>

Pushing and shoving with SEPHY *not able to retaliate?*

<u>I can't believe you're a Cross!</u>

The physical assault escalates –

<u>blank</u> face blank mind bitter Blanker lover –

SEPHY *is held back by* LOLA *or* DIONNE *punches* SEPHY *in the face. She falls back but starts fighting back as best she can.*

MR BOWDEN *catches them.*

MR BOWDEN. <u>Stop this!</u>

The GIRLS *run off.* SEPHY *is crying.*

CALLUM. <u>I don't</u>.

RYAN *arrives back from work.*

JUDE. You know what I said to Lynny?

<u>Who do you think you are?</u> You're the same as me, Lynette. As white as me. And I think you know that – because if you really hated yourself as much as you say you'd do something. Die or something! Admit it: *you* <u>don't believe you're a Cross!</u> (*Shouting up the stairs.*) You know as well as me, that when people look at you they'll always see a <u>Blanker</u>!

Noise of banging upstairs.

CALLUM *shoves* JUDE – *they fight at the same time as the girls.*

RYAN. <u>Stop!</u> (*Grabs* JUDE.) Jude. I'm disgusted with you.

RYAN *calms himself down.*

Awkwardly, MR BOWDEN *hugs* SEPHY *as the following conversation happens.*

RYAN. Your poor sister, what she's been through –
Three years ago – when we said Lynette was visiting relatives – she was in hospital.
She was attacked, by our own.
By three Noughts. Left for dead. Because she'd been seeing a Cross boy.

CALLUM *(hostile, to* JUDE). Did you know this?

JUDE. No.

RYAN. We told you what we had to – because she didn't want you to know – but that's why she was away for so long. And that's why she can't bear to think of herself as one of us any more. Now you know, you leave her alone. Understand?

JUDE *does a small nod.* RYAN *goes to* LYNETTE.

SEPHY. Antiseptic fills my nose.
Watch so much TV a screen grows in my head.
Stuck in bed.
Stuck together with stitches.
Yet all I can think is –
is he okay? How was school for him today?
Where is my –

CALLUM *approaches the house.*

JASMINE. Callum.

CALLUM. Mrs Hadley. I heard what happened yesterday.
I didn't know, I... can I see Sephy, please?

JASMINE. As far as I'm aware, Callum, Sephy got beaten up at school yesterday for sticking up for you, and you repaid her loyalty by telling her to go away.

CALLUM. I never told her to go away! I said I wasn't her friend, which was a lie, a stupid lie to try and protect her. To stop this from happening.

JASMINE. Well, it did happen. Shame you didn't inherit your mother's values.

CALLUM. What do you mean?

JASMINE. About finding dignity in the truth. Just leave Persephone alone – you hear me? Go home. Don't come back here again.

CALLUM. Please. Please at least tell her I'm sorry –

JASMINE *exits*.

Home. Only homely thing about that house is talking to a closed door.

CALLUM *arrives back at his house. He sits by* LYNETTE*'s door*.

Lynny? You there?

There's an indication of her presence.

It's better to be in there than out here, I reckon. You've got the right idea. But I do miss you. Do you remember when we all used to play hide and seek downstairs? Drive Mum mad with messing up the lounge?

A reaction.

I'm sorry, Lynny. About what happened to you. I didn't know.
I don't know what I could've done if I did. But I hate the thought of you lying in a bed all bruised and –

A reaction. Stop.

Course. Sorry. Stupid of me to... I don't think I'm much use at the moment. As a brother, as a friend.

He puts his hand to the door. A note comes out the bottom. CALLUM *picks it up and reads it*.

'You are the best brother ever. Your heart holds up the world Callum, always follow it.' See – you manage to make me feel better when I came here to see how you were. Thanks, Lynny. *You're* the best. Night.

CALLUM *rests his head on* LYNETTE's *door.*

JASMINE *rests her head on* SEPHY's *door. She knocks lightly.*

JASMINE. Can I come in, Persephone?

SEPHY. You're in, aren't you?

JASMINE. How are you?

SEPHY. Has anyone called for me?

JASMINE. No, nobody.

SEPHY. Nobody?

JASMINE. No.

SEPHY. What about Dad?

JASMINE. I told Juno.

SEPHY. His PA?! So you two can't talk at all any more, even when one of your children is attacked?!

JASMINE. I tried. I don't like to burden you but really, he is *not* the man I married and –

SEPHY. Are you drunk, mother?

JASMINE. I've had a glass of wine, what's wrong with that?

Beat.

SEPHY. I'm tired now. Could you leave me, please?

JASMINE *is devastated. She nods. Leaves.* SEPHY *hears a sound. It's something at her window. Could it be – ? She tiptoes to the window and peers out.* CALLUM *is hanging precariously on the ledge.*

Callum!

CALLUM. Aren't you going to invite me in then?

SEPHY *opens the window wide. In the light,* CALLUM *is visibly upset by* SEPHY*'s cuts.*

Sorry, Sephy.

SEPHY. These are just cuts. You said in front of everybody that we weren't friends. There's no stitches for that, Callum.

CALLUM. I wanted to protect you. So I said something I shouldn't have. You know how that feels, don't you?

SEPHY. You're saying we're even now?

CALLUM. I'm just saying, I'm sorry. I'll never say anything so stupid again.

Beat. SEPHY *smiles.*

SEPHY. Why did you come all the way up here?

CALLUM. Your mum was *not* happy with me trying to see you.

SEPHY. She's not happy with anyone or anything except wine at the moment.

CALLUM. I went home when she told me to. Then Lynny wrote me a note saying to follow my heart and I thought, I want to. I really do. For Lynny. For you. So here I am. I've always been a good climber.

SEPHY. It means a lot that you came.

JASMINE (*off*). Don't treat me like this!

SEPHY. It's Mum, you better go –
If Mother catches you, she'll crush you into wine!
Please thank Lynny from me –

CALLUM *leaves.*

MINERVA *enters.*

JASMINE (*off*). Don't you dare.
Don't you dare walk away from me –

An argument which MINERVA *and* SEPHY *overhear.*

JASMINE. Don't treat me like this, Kamal – I won't stand for it!

KAMAL. Oh, please, you can't stand for anything, I'm surprised you can even stay upright.

JASMINE. So you're not even going to deny it?

KAMAL. Why should I? It's about time you and I faced the truth. Enough is enough.

JASMINE. *You* get to decide when it's time for the truth, do you? When it's 'enough'? Enough for *who* exactly? I've been a good wife to you. A good mother to our children.

KAMAL. Oh yes. You've been an excellent example of loyalty and dedication.

JASMINE. I've done my best.

KAMAL. Well, your best isn't up to much, Jasmine!

JASMINE. At least I was *here*. I was *here*, Kamal.

Beat.

I wanted us to try… to start again.

KAMAL. Jasmine, look at us, look at yourself – we are long past starting again.

JASMINE. You're a cruel man.

KAMAL. And you're a drunk.

JASMINE. Then get out so I can drink a toast to watching the man I made walk away like the coward he is.

JASMINE stares at KAMAL. He shakes his head and walks out.

She goes the opposite way.

MINERVA. Dad's got someone else.

SEPHY. You don't know that.

MINERVA. Weren't you listening?

SEPHY. No – it's just her – driving him away with all her funny moods.

MINERVA. You seriously live your life blindfolded! Do you ever really see anything? Sometimes, Sephy, I don't think you'll ever grow up and – well, lucky you, I hope you don't have to.

Beat.

SEPHY. You all seem to think I'm already grown up enough to have to look after myself around here, so thank you for –

MINERVA *leaves in a huff.*

(*Calling after her.*) Everything isn't my fault!

MEGGIE *and* RYAN *are arguing at the table.*

MEGGIE. It's not about that, Ryan.
(*To* CALLUM – *multitasking.*) Hey, where do you think you've been? See if your sister's finished her dinner – (*To* RYAN.) It's that any change which comes about through violence isn't really change, just more of the same and –

RYAN. You're wrong, Meggie. Now, I'm not a violent man, as you know. But – no change at all happens without violence, in the whole history of the world, so –

By 'No change at all – ' CALLUM *has reached* LYNETTE*'s door. It is open. He is in shock. There's nobody there. There is a letter for him.*

CALLUM (*shouting*). Lynny's gone!

RYAN *and* MEGGIE *stop arguing.*

MEGGIE. I can't understand it. Lynny hasn't been outside in over a year.

CALLUM. I'm sure she'll be back soon, Mum.

JUDE. I'm gonna go round the block one more time to see –

JUDE *meets a* POLICE OFFICER *on his way out of the house.*

POLICE. The McGregors?

MEGGIE. Yes –

POLICE. Your daughter – She's – we –
    We've found her –

   POLICE OFFICER *gives* RYAN *something of* LYNETTE*'s.*

RYAN. Identity card. It's her / identity card.

POLICE. / Her body.

RYAN. What did you say?

POLICE. We think we've found her body. I'm very sorry. We
    think she was hit. On the motorway. I am so sorry. An
    accident. We need you to identify –

CALLUM. Lynny.

RYAN. No.

JUDE. Lynny.

MEGGIE. My baby. My baby. My baby.

POLICE. It was immediate. No pain. Nobody's fault.

MEGGIE. My baby.

RYAN. Nobody's fault.

MEGGIE. My baby.

JUDE. Nobody's fault.

MEGGIE. My baby!

RYAN. Nobody's fault.

   JASMINE *enters and takes an overdose.*

CALLUM. LYNNY!!!!

   MINERVA *finds* JASMINE.

MINERVA. SEPHY, PHONE FOR AN AMBULANCE NOW!

SEPHY *is sitting beside her mother, who is in a hospital bed, and* MINERVA *sits beside her.* SEPHY *tentatively strokes her mother's hair and looks to* MINERVA, *worried.*

MINERVA *is on the phone.*

MINERVA. How dare you, Juno, when our mother has just –
     Of course we had to phone an ambulance.
     Why should *we* care if it's on the news!

     Hangs up.

     I can't believe this. I can't believe he isn't here. I can't
     believe I have to speak to his PA when Mum is lying here in
     hospital.

     (*Impersonates Juno on the phone.*) 'You should have rang
     me first. The papers are all over this, saying Kamal Hadley's
     wife attempts suicide because he has a mistress – She just
     wanted attention or she'd have taken a *proper* overdose.
     Well, suppose she's got attention now – '

SEPHY. She never said that!

     MINERVA *nods.*

MINERVA. I hate him. I *hate* him.

SEPHY. Me too. I think.

     A moment between them as sisters.

     I just want her to wake up.

MINERVA. The doctor said she'll be fine.

SEPHY. Minnie… I know she also had an… did something to
     make Dad mad all those years ago, and I know how unhappy
     she is, I just never thought… I never imagined she…

     MINERVA *nods and they hug – it is the first time for a long
     time.*

     CALLUM *is holding the letter from* LYNETTE. *He hesitates
     and opens it.*

CALLUM. 'My dear Callum.

You are good and golden and growing as a person, while the
rest of our family shrinks. Don't think I hate them. I love you
all. But this is only for you. I know now that I'm not a Cross.
I knew from when Jude shouted louder than a storm. And the
truth is harder for me to take than being in a cloud. So I'm
going out and I'm going to find a way to make my end look
like an accident. Let them all think it was an accident.
Please. I want you to know the truth because I believe you
will choose to do something good in this life and the truth
will help you to do that. I love you always, Lynny.'
Lynny, Lynny.

CALLUM *rips up the letter.*

Time passes with the families.

SEPHY. When Mum came home, her drinking got worse not
better.
The whole of that winter there was no let-up.
Every day she stumbled, fumbled for words.
The whole house hurt, Minerva was back to her curt, cold
self.
Dad told us all he was officially moving out –
though not officially enough to go public, of course.
By now it was as though my family only spoke in Morse code.
I needed to talk to someone. Callum, who else?
But every time I tried, the words wouldn't come,
As if he wasn't going through enough with Lynny gone.
So I kept it all zipped up.

CALLUM. That winter, not a moment passed
without me thinking about Lynette. What she did. Why.
What could I have done?
Was… was being a Nought really enough to make her want
to die?
And what did that mean for those of us still alive?
Then I felt bad for thinking that.
Jude and Dad weren't around much any more

or when they were, it was whispers galore.
No more 'live and let live' – that's what Dad swore
as Lynny's ashes floated up with the frothing sea.
And Mum? Not much came out of her mouth now.
I needed to talk to someone. Sephy, who else?
But every time I tried, the words wouldn't come,
she was going through enough with her own mum.
So I kept it all zipped up.
Until –

CALLUM *calls* SEPHY *with the coded ring from his house phone to hers.*

SEPHY. Hi, Callum.

CALLUM. Hello, you.

SEPHY. I wondered if you'd forgotten my number.

CALLUM. Never. I tried a few times, either nobody answered or I got your housekeeper picking up and shouting about nuisance calls.

They laugh.

SEPHY. I still can't believe that Lynette… I know I don't have the words to say how – and I should have, I should have –

CALLUM. It's all right, Sephy. You've had your mum to deal with.

Beat.

How you doing, anyway?

SEPHY. I'm all right. You? I feel like I never see you at school.

CALLUM. Trying to keep my head down, get those grades up.

SEPHY. Is it working?

CALLUM. You're talking to Heathcroft's straight-A student right now.

SEPHY. Callum, that's great, I'm so proud! Carry on like that and you might be the first Nought to get to university!

CALLUM. Yeah. Maybe. You up for hanging out? It's Saturday, and –

SEPHY. I'd love to but – just about to go shopping with Mother. Urgh.

CALLUM. Your favourite pastime, ay?

SEPHY. I guess it's better than her sitting in drinking, but it'll just be shoe shop after shoe shop. Like 'Ooh electric blue ones with a little orange stripe, or dark blue ones with a little burgundy dot, or baby blue ones with silver buckles?' and I'll be like, 'Mum, you don't even go out!'

CALLUM. I got to get a new calculator actually. It's a shame you can't come with me. You could have compared calculators with me – the black one with the slate-grey case? Or the slate-grey one with the black case?

They laugh.

SEPHY. For something that life-changing I'll find a way to sneak off. See you in the Cuckoo Café at one?

CALLUM. I'm not allowed in a Cross café.

SEPHY. It's all right, you'll be with me.

CALLUM. No, Sephy, I can't. I'll meet you outside.

SEPHY. Okay. See you there at one.

They put the phone down, happy. CALLUM *gets his coat on.* JUDE *appears.*

JUDE. Off out?

CALLUM. Why do you care?

JUDE. Don't. Just asking.

CALLUM. I'm going to Dundale Shopping / Centre –

JUDE. No – you're staying in.

JUDE *gets hold of* CALLUM.

MEGGIE. Jude, what are you doing?

CALLUM. Get off me, Jude – what are you – ?

JUDE. Listen to me – you are not to go anywhere near that place today.

MEGGIE. Jude!

Pause. It sinks in that this is to do with the Liberation Militia.

CALLUM. What have you done?

JUDE. Just stay away from there. Stay. Away.

MEGGIE. Jude –

CALLUM. Sephy, shit –

CALLUM *runs off.*

JUDE. Callum!

MEGGIE. Jude, what have you done?

SEPHY *is sipping orange juice. Looking around. She sees* CALLUM *running towards her, out of breath, and she smiles and waves.*

SEPHY. Perfect timing, Mother's gone to put the shopping in the car, you can't imagine / how –

CALLUM. Sephy, we have to go, now. *Now.*

CALLUM *is pulling a confused* SEPHY.

CROSS MAN. Is this young man bothering you, miss?

SEPHY. No, no, he's my friend. Callum, what's – ?

CALLUM. Do you trust me?

SEPHY. With my life.

CALLUM. Then when I say we have to run, run: *run*!

They run. There's a huge explosion –

CALLUM *and* SEPHY *are thrown to the ground.*

Screaming. Silence. Sirens. Then –

Are you all right?

SEPHY. I… I think so. Are you?

CALLUM. Fine, I think.

SEPHY. What just happened…?

CALLUM *shakes his head.*

Oh my God – Mother, I've got to check she's okay.

She hugs CALLUM *and runs off.*

Chaos remains on stage.

The families watch video bites of the aftermath of the bomb. A cacophony, all running into each other. During this, SEPHY *secretly gets and drinks a bottle of wine.*

JOURNALIST. Seven people have been killed in the Dundale Shopping Centre bombing, and countless injured.

JOURNALIST. There was a warning given by the Liberation Militia just five minutes before the explosion.

KAMAL (*being interviewed*). Families of the deceased have been informed and we will not stop until these terrorists have been brought to justice.

The McGREGORS'. *The family circle each other.*

MEGGIE. I want the truth.

RYAN. There's nothing to say, Meggie.

MEGGIE. The truth. Jude, look at me, not at Callum, not at your dad. Me, your mother. The truth, Jude.

RYAN. Jude…

JUDE. They said there'd be a proper warning, that everyone would be evacuated. Dad, you said – you said –

MEGGIE *stops for a moment, changing the pace, retching.*

MEGGIE. Oh my God. Murderers.

RYAN. This is a war, Meggie.

MEGGIE. You promised me there'd never be anything like this. You promised me, you'd only be in the background!

CALLUM. What the hell is going on? You were all in on this!?

JUDE. Dad, what happened?

RYAN. They said they'd send a warning, I don't know why they didn't. It was legitimate action – think of what we're trying to achieve here – basic rights to a decent life! Think of Lynny.

MEGGIE *stops, steps to* RYAN *and slaps him so hard she hurts her finger.*

MEGGIE. I think of my daughter every single day and this is beyond an insult to her memory. I do not want to speak to you ever again, Ryan McGregor.

RYAN. We have to stick together now.

JUDE. Mum –

MEGGIE (*to* RYAN). You've been brainwashed.

RYAN. You're the one who's been brainwashed! Believing you can just try hard, be good, be honest, and you'll be able to live your life well and in peace –

MEGGIE. Oh, so murder is the way forward, is it?

RYAN. It went wrong. We only wanted a way to a better world for our children, Meggie.

MEGGIE. I want you to get out of my house, Ryan.

CALLUM. Mum!

RYAN. It's my house too.

MEGGIE. You've dragged my sons into all this!

JUDE. I dragged *him* into it, Mum. If he leaves this house then
so do I.

Pause.

MEGGIE. Fine. If both of you leaving is what it takes to keep
Callum safe, then so be it.

RYAN. Meggie?

MEGGIE. Don't touch me. I want you out by tonight.

MEGGIE *leaves and* RYAN *follows.*

SEPHY. Can't sleep. Can't rest.
Something to switch it all off,
to make me forget –

*She takes wine from the fridge and drinks and drinks and
drinks.*

Spins onto the beach, meeting CALLUM.

Well, hello, good sir!

CALLUM. You're drunk?

SEPHY. This way – come ooonnnn –
Come on, dance with me! Dance with me ooooh dance –

CALLUM *twists around to hold* SEPHY's *shoulders.*

CALLUM. Stop it, Sephy. You're completely pissed and it's not
fun, all right, just stop it.

SEPHY. Ooooh, yes, sir…

She makes an attempt to kiss CALLUM *but he pushes her
away.*

CALLUM. What's wrong with you?

SEPHY. I have taken a liking to wine and cider, dear sir – it
helps me.

CALLUM. Helps you be an idiot?

SEPHY. Shut up!

CALLUM. Are you trying to be like your mum? At least she
has an excuse – what's yours? Wait, did your driver drop you
on the wrong side of the road?

SEPHY. In case you've forgotten, we were just in a bombing!
Where people were killed!

CALLUM. I just came to say that –

Beat.

SEPHY. Do you ever stop to think what this life is like for me?
Everyone either openly hates me or secretly hates me. All
mapped out. 'Just be a good girl, Sephy, make no mistakes,
Sephy, smile for the fucking camera, Sephy.' You say your
life's bad, well, I can't do anything I want to do either, you
know!

She makes to leave.

CALLUM. Wait.

SEPHY. Get lost, Callum!

CALLUM. Sephy –

SEPHY. Go back to the LM!

CALLUM. What?

SEPHY (*softly*). How did you know, Callum? About the bomb?
How did you know?

CALLUM *kisses* SEPHY *and this time it is serious. They are
both totally in it.*

CALLUM. I've got to go…

SEPHY. Callum!

Back at the McGREGORS'.

JUDE *and* RYAN *are leaving.*

MEGGIE *and* RYAN *have no more words for one another.*

RYAN. Bye, son.
Look after your mum, all right.
It's all on you now.
(*To* JUDE.) Stay safe, Jude.

CALLUM (*to* RYAN). Where you going?

RYAN. Aunt Amanda's – a few nights – get my head together, then… I don't know. I'll be in touch. (*To* JUDE.) Are you sure you're going to be / all right?

JUDE. I'll be fine, Dad.

CALLUM. Sticking with the LM. After they lied to you.

JUDE. They didn't lie.

Beat.

RYAN. Right then.

He leaves.

JUDE *makes to leave.*

CALLUM. Jude, where will you be?

JUDE. Like you care.

CALLUM. I do care. You're my brother.

JUDE. I'll be fighting for a better world.

CALLUM. What, by killing people?

JUDE. Noughts are dying, Callum. That's why this is a war. And why this is the first thing I've ever been part of that I'm proud to be a part of, and nothing will make me leave it, not you and your bleeding heart, not even Mum.

RYAN *and* JUDE *leave.* CALLUM *and* MEGGIE *watch.*

JASMINE *holding an empty bottle.*

JASMINE. Persephone – what was this doing in your room?

Beat.

SEPHY. It was just a swig.

JASMINE. Sephy – this is an empty bottle of wine.

SEPHY. Only one bottle.

JASMINE. This is dangerous.

SEPHY. And you should know –

Beat.

It was just something I tried.

JASMINE. Sephy…

SEPHY. I won't take your wine again, okay!

JASMINE. This is not about taking my wine! You are a child. My child. This is not for you. Do you understand?

SEPHY. Yes.

Beat.

JASMINE. Sephy, after last week, what you're going through, what you must be feeling, it's natural to be… you know… but –

SEPHY. I can't get it out of my head, Mum.

JASMINE. I know. We were very lucky.

SEPHY. Are we always just lucky, or is there more to it, Mum? Maybe they were right, what they did?

JASMINE. There is never anything right about violence, Sephy.

SEPHY. You tried to kill yourself.

JASMINE. I…

SEPHY. I need to get away.

JASMINE. What?

SEPHY. I need to get away from here. From that school.

JASMINE. No, I don't think that's the answer.

SEPHY. Mum, lots of people go to boarding school.

JASMINE. Boarding school? But your place is here, with me.

SEPHY. Please, Mum – you'll still have Minnie, and the staff and your parties.

JASMINE. No, Sephy.

SEPHY. Please. I want to focus on my studies without distractions. If I don't go, I know things will get worse, Mum, much, much worse, and you won't want to think back and know you could've helped me when I asked you to, so please / just –

JASMINE. It's a big decision, Sephy. Leave it with me.

CALLUM *gets to his house. He starts coughing and stumbling. There are shouts from the* POLICE (*as many or few as is possible for the company*) –

CALLUM. What's going on? I can't see anything –
Mum, are you home?

POLICE. Stay right there! Hands behind your head! Get on the floor! Stand up! Move!

CALLUM. Where are you taking me?

CALLUM *is now taken to a police station or interview room, as the questions continue seamlessly.*

POLICE. Where is your brother? Where's your dad?

CALLUM. I don't know. Where's my mum?

POLICE. Do you hate us Crosses? Do you hate us Crosses? Do you hate us Crosses?

CALLUM. I don't hate anyone, just tell me what is going on, please?!

POLICE. One more time, tell us about your family –

CALLUM. Where's my mum?!

There is a call. The POLICE *murmur and nod.*

POLICE. You can go.

    CALLUM *is almost thrown into* MEGGIE*'s arms.*

MEGGIE. Callum! Thank God you're all right, my love.
They've got your dad. They're gonna charge him with
political terrorism and... and seven counts of murder.

CALLUM. What?

KELANI. Kelani Adams QC – the good news is I'll take your
husband's case.

MEGGIE. Thank you, but – we haven't got any money.

KELANI. It's been taken care of. Your benefactor wanted the
best, a world-renowned barrister. But it's not about the
money. I've read the file. Unfortunately, Jude's fingerprints
have been found on a drink can near the bomb.

    MEGGIE *and* CALLUM *are upset at this revelation.*

I suspect the police have used this to get Ryan to sign a
confession.

It's obvious he's protecting his son.

CALLUM. Oh God, oh God. Um. Okay. Thank you. But...
What do you mean 'benefactor', who – ?

KELANI. I was contacted by an anonymous donor. If I
represent you, the terms of the agreement state their identity
must remain secret. Do you want to proceed? It may be your
only chance for your husband to emerge from this a free
man.

    MEGGIE *and* CALLUM *look at each other and nod.*

You will both be cross-examined in the trial. I will prepare
you as best I can – but from this moment, you need to agree
to tell me everything.

    They nod.

First of all, do either of you know where Jude is?

MEGGIE/CALLUM. No.

KELANI. Good, keep it that way.

    CALLUM *steps out.*

CALLUM. Jude *planted* the bomb?
    Jude *planted* the bomb?
    No, that can't be right! It's…
    Jude planted the bomb.
    Oh shit, Dad. *Dad!*
    My family is so far down it's like being inside the core of the earth,
    all molten and muddy and no space to see clear or breathe clear –
    Breathe, Callum. Breathe.

A courtroom. SEPHY *paces. She peers around for* CALLUM.

SEPHY. Breathe, Sephy, breathe.
    They say it's the trial of the century.
    To be judged by twelve good Cross men and women.
    Because only Cross men and women can be 'good', right?
    This world, my world, it makes me sick.
    I don't believe your dad did it, Callum,
    but I also know you knew more than you should've.
    Your face.
    Calm Callum, even now, with all this.
    My heart breaks for you…

    RYAN *in the defendant box.* MEGGIE *and* CALLUM *are there, and so are* SEPHY *and* JASMINE. *The prosecutor,* MR PINGULE, *and* KELANI *are already in front of* JUDGE ANDERSON.

    KELANI *nods to* CALLUM, *he takes the witness box and a chunky copy of 'the good book' is placed under his hand.*

VOICE-OVER. All rise for the Honourable Judge Anderson.

JUDGE ANDERSON. You may be seated. Do you swear to tell the truth, the whole truth and nothing but the truth?

CALLUM. I do.

JUDGE ANDERSON. Could you state your full name for the record, please?

CALLUM. Callum Ryan McGregor.

JUDGE ANDERSON. Mr Pingule, for the prosecution, you may begin.

PINGULE. Thank you, Your Honour. Callum Ryan McGregor, Can I call you Callum?

CALLUM. Yes.

PINGULE. Do you belong to the Liberation Militia, Callum?

KELANI. I object, Your Honour. Callum McGregor is sixteen and he is not on trial here.

PINGULE. It goes to witness credibility, Your Honour.

JUDGE ANDERSON. I'll allow it.

PINGULE. Do you belong to the Liberation Militia, / Callum?

CALLUM. No, I don't.

PINGULE. You do not?

CALLUM. No.

PINGULE. What's your opinion on the LM?

KELANI. Your Honour, objection –

JUDGE ANDERSON. Overruled. This means you must answer the question, Mr McGregor.

Pause.

CALLUM. I… I think… my opinion is that Noughts and Crosses should be equal, so I guess, I agree with that aim but I don't agree with violence, so I'm not sure, completely.

PINGULE. You're not completely sure you can condemn the Liberation Militia as terrorists, then?

KELANI. Your Honour –

PINGULE. Withdrawn. Did your father ever mention belonging to or joining the LM?

CALLUM. No.

PINGULE. Did your brother ever mention belonging to or joining the LM?

CALLUM. No.

PINGULE. So no one in your family had anything to do with the planting of the bomb at the Dundale Shopping Centre?

KELANI. Your Honour, my learned colleague has been asking the same question for ten minutes. If he has a point, perhaps he could get to it soon?

PINGULE. Your Honour, I call into evidence Exhibit D19.

A screen appears.

KELANI. I strenuously object, Your Honour, I have not been notified of this exhibit –

PINGULE. Your Honour, this is a tape from the day of the bombing. I only acquired it last night and consider it of the utmost importance.

KELANI. Your Honour, there are precedents to presenting evidence in court not yet seen by the defence. If I can quote –

JUDGE ANDERSON. I am aware of the precedents... you are not the only one who went to law school, Ms Adams. Considering the urgency, I will allow this evidence.

The screen starts to play the moment in which CALLUM *rushes into the café to drag* SEPHY *out. They run out of the frame and the bomb goes off just after. Everyone watches/partakes in the scene as* CALLUM *and* SEPHY *watch each other, shocked.*

There is a silence after the video ends.

PINGULE. Callum, do you still insist that neither you nor any member of your family knew anything about the planting of the bomb at the Dundale Shopping Centre?

CALLUM. Yes.

PINGULE. I see. In the film, who were you pulling from the Cuckoo Café?

CALLUM. Sephy... Persephone Hadley...

And everything spins till we land with...

SEPHY *in the witness box.*

PINGULE. What happened when you were in the Cuckoo Café on the day of the bombing?

JUDGE ANDERSON. Take your time, Miss Hadley.

SEPHY. I was having a drink in the café. Mother... My mother had gone back to the car to put away our shopping...

PINGULE. Go on.

SEPHY. Um. Callum came in, we had... we had arranged to meet so I waved him over. He said we had to leave.

PINGULE. Why? Did he give you a reason why you had to leave the café?

SEPHY. He... he wanted to show me something... outside.

PINGULE. What did he want to show you outside?

SEPHY. I don't know. I mean, he said it was a surprise but then... the bomb went off.

PINGULE. And that, Miss Hadley, is the truth?

SEPHY. Yes.

She steps down.

The verdict. It's happening.

CALLUM. Me and Mum hold hands, still can't believe this is happening.

JUDGE ANDERSON. Do you find the defendant, Ryan Callum McGregor, guilty or not guilty –

SEPHY. The head of the jury stands up –

CALLUM. But I can't hear –

Action goes into slow motion – reactions to the verdict of 'Guilty.'

SEPHY (*softly*). Callum!

CALLUM *collapses.*

A public execution is set up. SEPHY *is there with her family.*

SEPHY. Oh no. Not this. How could you – ?

SEPHY *starts leaving.*

KAMAL. Sephy, sit down. I'll be back in a minute.

He leaves.

SEPHY. Mum – Mum – let's leave.

JASMINE. Not now, Sephy!

SEPHY. Minnie?

MINERVA. Sit down.

SEPHY. I'm going!

MINERVA. Stop being so / dramatic, Sephy –

SEPHY. Dramatic? Not wanting to watch a murder?

JASMINE. Stay where you are.

SEPHY. You're enjoying this, aren't you?

JASMINE. Persephone! Come with me.

Taking her slightly out of MINERVA*'s earshot.*

The McGregors were my friends once. I am as upset about this as you are.

SEPHY. The only thing you get upset about is spilling wine.

JASMINE *slaps* SEPHY.

JASMINE. Who do you think paid for the McGregors' lawyer, Persephone? I did what I could, how I could, now be quiet.

SEPHY *shocked, holding her face.*

MEGGIE (*looking over at* JASMINE). This all started with her lies. Your father was right. I've been naive. This is a war, Callum.

RYAN *is brought out, with an* EXECUTIONER *wearing a hood – and put on the scaffold.*

The clock is striking. First strike, RYAN *nods to* CALLUM *and* MEGGIE. *Second, loud weeping sounds. Third, a hood goes over* RYAN*'s head. Fourth,* RYAN *shouts:*

RYAN. Long live the Liberation Militia!

The EXECUTIONER *hesitates.*

JASMINE. What's happening?

The PRISON GOVERNOR *appears.*

GOVERNOR. As the Governor of this prison, I announce that the execution is stayed. I repeat. The execution is stayed.

Silence. The hood is taken off RYAN. *He is confused, as is everyone else, except* KAMAL.

Mr McGregor's sentence has been changed to life imprisonment, by the mercy of the Home Secretary, Kamal Hadley. No hanging today.

RYAN *collapses, a* PRISON OFFICER *has to hold him.*

Sounds of a riot mixed with sounds of cheering.

MEGGIE (*enraged*). A political stunt? With my Ryan's life?

JASMINE (*relieved*). A reprieve!

SEPHY. Thank God!

They stand in the quiet, in front of a deflated RYAN *and the*
OFFICER.

MEGGIE. I'm grateful you're alive, Ryan.

RYAN. I'm not.

MEGGIE. Ryan –

RYAN. I was ready to die. I am ready to die for what I believe
in – equality, fairness, justice. I'm not so ready to rot in
prison for the rest of my life for those things. Maybe that
makes no sense to you, but death feels like an action,
something I've done, to help, to have an impact. Being a
prisoner, well that's just –

CALLUM. *We* need you here, alive. Dad?

MEGGIE. Don't give up, Ryan, we can appeal, we can still do
lots of things, Kelani says –

RYAN. I don't want any of you to do anything more. If there's a
way out of here, I'll find it myself.

MEGGIE. Ryan, don't be doing anything stupid.

RYAN. I've got it all figured out, Meggie, don't you worry.

SEPHY. Callum!

CALLUM. Sephy.

SEPHY. I had to see you. I know your dad didn't do it.

CALLUM. Me and you, Sephy, we're done. It's all too – look at
this, what's happening because of me and you. If I hadn't
met you and they didn't have that video. Just – goodbye.
Mum, let's go!

Later, CALLUM *goes to* SEPHY's *bedroom – entering through
the window again.*

SEPHY *has been crying.*

SEPHY (*softly*). Callum. What… Why are you here?

Beat. CALLUM *shrugs.*

How's your mum?

CALLUM. At my aunt's.

SEPHY. I'm so sorr–

CALLUM. Sorry sorry sorry. That's all you ever have to say.

SEPHY. What do you want me to say? What do you want me to do?

CALLUM. At least stop pretending to care.

SEPHY. At least stop pretending you don't hate me.

Beat.

You *hate* me.
You've hated me since I said that word.

CALLUM. You've hated me since I didn't defend you at school.

SEPHY. I don't. I could *never* hate you.

CALLUM. You hated me enough to come and watch my dad die.

SEPHY. My dad forced me to come!

Beat.

Callum, I know this is all beyond messed up and there's so many lies everywhere and we were always honest to each other, before, so I just want to say… I think you're here because you know I… I'll always have love for you and… you will for me too, no matter how much gets thrown at us.

Beat.

CALLUM. Love doesn't exist. Friendship doesn't exist. Not between a Nought and a Cross. Not for us.

He is upset.

SEPHY. I wish I could be somebody else, Callum, but I can't.

Pause.

CALLUM. I used to think that one day, we could maybe go away together. I know it's stupid. When I can't even have a passport. Just somewhere. Anywhere.

SEPHY. I wish you'd have said that to me before.

CALLUM. Before what?

SEPHY. I'm leaving, Callum.

CALLUM. Leaving?

SEPHY. I'm going to boarding school. With all this going on, Mum and Dad agreed in the end it's the best place for me. I want to be a better person, after what you said about me ending up like Mother, and, well…

CALLUM. When are you… going?

SEPHY. Tomorrow night.

CALLUM. The privilege of a Cross – just leave when things get too much.

CALLUM *starts to leave.*

SEPHY. Please try to understand – Callum?

He's gone.

KAMAL. Despite the kindness shown by this Government,
and by me in particular as Home Secretary,
Ryan Callum McGregor,
the convicted bomber of the Dundale Shopping Centre,
was killed this evening whilst trying to escape from
Hewmett Prison.
He attempted to scale the electrified security fence.
He was electrocuted as a result of his actions.
We are, of course, incredibly sad to learn he did not
appreciate the gift he was given by this Government.

Please be assured that we have launched an immediate inquiry into the incident.
We are still searching high and low for his son, Jude McGregor,
for questioning in relation to the bombing.
Stay alert, everyone.
We are all responsible for the safety of this country.

CALLUM *roars*.

End of Act One.

ACT TWO

ENSEMBLE. When a handwritten letter arrives
    it means there's hope
    or
    it means there's disaster, right?
    Keep it sealed to keep the hope in
    or
    rip it open, there's no more hiding.

    CALLUM *and* SEPHY *have letters.*

SEPHY. Three years ago
    I gave up on childish dreams,
    on being someone who could survive
    in the toxicity of this city.
    Ran to Chivers boarding school
    and never came back – until now.
    Seeing this godforsaken place,
    I have to work hard to keep those surfacing
    memories from overwhelming me.
    The day I left, I thought I'd left it all behind me,
    but I still see it so clearly –

    Flashback: SEPHY *and* MEGGIE.

    Please give him this. I'm leaving tonight. Please will you
    give it to him? I risked such a lot to find you. I only wanted
    him to know – I only wanted to say this –

    MEGGIE *takes the letter.*

CALLUM. Three years ago
    I gave up on childish dreams,
    on being someone who could survive,
    rise above whatever this messed-up society
    decided I had to be.
    Ran away to the shadows

and never came back – until now.
Seeing this godforsaken place,
the memories sway through my veins like waves –

Flashback: CALLUM *and* JUDE.

Jude! Oh my –

CALLUM *hugs* JUDE, JUDE *pulls away.*

JUDE. Stop grinning like an idiot.

CALLUM. Bro.

JUDE. Let's keep our heads down, okay?

CALLUM. You know… about Dad?

JUDE. Yeah. How's Mum?

CALLUM. She's… pretty bad, Jude.

JUDE. I hear they booted you out of Heathcroft.

CALLUM. I walked.

JUDE. Good. Need to be somewhere you can make a
difference.
With me, *us.*

Beat.

Do you want in, Callum?

Beat.

In or out. It's a yes or no.

CALLUM. I guess… yeah. Yes.

JUDE. Let's go.

CALLUM. Three years since I started training.
Liberation Militia teaboy, at first.
Once they have you, they don't let you go –
my dad said that.
So now here I am, rose through the ranks –

Does training exercises.

– to become Sergeant McGregor.
Sold my soul, lost it, for a lot of things, some good, some bad.

Fighting, shooting.

Got back those girls who beat up Sephy, got them good, bad.
Hadn't seen my mum since I left. Till today.
Left her in a cloud of sadness, found her in a storm.
Spinning, alone. Still holding on to this letter.
Why give it to me now, all these years later?
This writing, I know it, Sephy's.
Sealed, so there's still hope.
I won't open it.
Disaster is already here.

SEPHY. Three years since I started boarding school.
　　Tough times at first, everything so swirling and new.
　　The deep ache of Callum not responding to my letter,
　　not making any contact whatsoever after all I wrote,
　　that ache smashed into this unknown world of Chivers
　　making my head and heart spill over
　　till
　　the drink did too.
　　I couldn't get out or in to bed without wine,
　　cider, gin, whatever I could find.
　　The other girls, though, they were kind.
　　They became my family, my rehab, my therapy.
　　My solidarity sisters who taught me
　　about the depth of disaster Crosses
　　had caused across the world with our supremacy
　　and I learnt all I could and promised I would do all I could
　　to be effective as possible against this system with peaceful –

CALLUM. Resistance.
　　Mum was resistant to even hug me, her youngest son.
　　Can't blame her. What we've done…
　　Wasn't even supposed to see her, my superiors said.
　　But I had to.

SEPHY/CALLUM (*holding their letters up*). I never expected
　　to get – this –

SEPHY. A note from Callum in my mail at home,
      his big wobbly writing saying he's heard I'm back
      for the summer so could we catch up?
      I've not got a clue what he's been doing,
      there's no undoing the past –
      he made a choice to cut me off
      and now I'm making one to say
      we can be friends again – why not?
      No matter what, old friends stay in the soul, don't they?

CALLUM. Hello, Sephy.

SEPHY. Hey, Callum. How are you?

CALLUM. All right. You?

SEPHY. Good. Great, actually. It's been –

CALLUM. Three years.

SEPHY. Yeah, a lifetime.

CALLUM. Yeah.

SEPHY. Um, I was surprised to get your note.

CALLUM. Sorry.

SEPHY. No, I mean good surprised. I've thought about you a
      lot these past years, I mean… It's just –

CALLUM. Sorry, Sephy, I'm sorry.

      CALLUM *leans forward to kiss her quickly on the cheek and
      as he does so,* JUDE *and a few other* NOUGHTS *capture
      her.* SEPHY *screams and they drag her off, leaving*
      CALLUM *to strengthen his resolve and follow them.*

REPORTER. Breaking news just in: Persephone Hadley, the
      daughter of Home Secretary Kamal Hadley, has been
      kidnapped by the Liberation Militia and is being held to
      ransom. This video of her was leaked just moments ago –

SEPHY (*on screen*). Dad, you'll never see me again unless you do exactly as you're told. Your instructions will be in the envelope along with this tape. You have twenty-four hours to follow their demands to the letter. If you don't, I'll be killed.

REPORTER. The video is thought to have been leaked by a member of Mr Hadley's private staff, but there is currently no information on the demands made, and Mr Hadley has made himself unavailable for comment at this time. We will keep you updated on this shocking story as it develops.

JUDE, CALLUM *and a few other* NOUGHTS *are standing in an underground hideaway.* SEPHY *is sitting on the floor in a cell and the others are outside the door.*

On a screen, they see KAMAL *hand in his notice.*

KAMAL (*on screen*). My decision to temporarily step down from office is purely so I can dedicate my immediate energies to finding and rescuing my daughter, Persephone. I have no further comment at this time.

JUDE. Good work, team, look at that, the first demand has been met, Kamal Hadley is out of office!

Whoops. High-fives.

ANDREW. A bit early to be celebrating, isn't it?

MORGAN. Password now, or I'll shoot.

ANDREW. Golden man.

MORGAN. You're the second-in-command?

ANDREW. Do you want to make something of it? So this is the famous stiletto unit? So far the General's not impressed. This is far from over. We've had a few sweets from the bowl but now the police and media know...

JUDE. But –

ANDREW. Callum McGregor, isn't it? I'm going to leave it to you to decide.

CALLUM. To decide what?

JUDE. How serious we are.

CALLUM. We're in an underground bunker in the middle of
the woods, risking our lives and freedom for this to go right.
I'd say it's obvious how serious we are, Jude.

JUDE. Callum, watch your tone.

ANDREW. Give us something to send by the time we leave, ten
minutes and counting…

JUDE *hands* CALLUM *some scissors. The others turn away
to get busy on something else.*

JUDE. You might be Mum's favourite, but remember, we're
doing this for Dad, so don't let us down, understand?

CALLUM *grabs* JUDE *by the shirt and puts the scissors to
his neck.*

CALLUM. And don't you doubt my loyalty, do *you*
understand?

JUDE. Ah, so the mouse can roar?

CALLUM. Do you understand?

JUDE. I understand.

CALLUM *lets him go.* CALLUM *gives* JUDE *the finger
behind his back and goes into the cell.* SEPHY *has glimpsed*
ANDREW*'s boots.*

CALLUM. Can you – take your top off, please.

SEPHY. Piss off, Callum.

CALLUM. Do it or I'll have to do it for you.

SEPHY. You've got scissors, if you need something of mine,
just cut the bottom bit off.

CALLUM. Fine.

CALLUM *is cutting her top at the bottom, very close to her,
she almost wants to stroke his hair.*

SEPHY. I recognise that voice that told you to do it, I'm sure
I do –

CALLUM. You don't, Sephy.

SEPHY. Are you going to kill me, Callum?

CALLUM. Just be quiet now, please.

SEPHY. That night I was drunk at the beach and we kissed, my
God I adored you so much.

Pause.

I'm sorry about your dad, Callum. I wanted him to live.

CALLUM. Every Cross is responsible for his death. Including
you.

SEPHY. So I deserve to die too, do I? For being a Cross?

CALLUM. That's up to your dad now.

SEPHY. Will you do it? Will you? Will it make you feel better
to stick those scissors in my neck? You kissed my neck once.

CALLUM. I'll follow my orders when the time comes.

SEPHY. And there you have it, I'm a Dagger bitch and you,
Callum, are a psycho Blanker bastard –

CALLUM *grabs* SEPHY*'s hand and cuts her finger with the
scissors, she gasps and cries.*

CALLUM. Um, sorry, I…

CALLUM *composes himself and wipes the blood on the bit
of her top he has cut off.* SEPHY *is sucking her finger.*

SEPHY. Will that impress big brother Jude?

Beat.

Your mum must be so proud, Callum.

CALLUM *is furious, but just stares and leaves.*

CALLUM *hands the piece of* SEPHY*'s top to* ANDREW. *The others are there too, about to leave.*

ANDREW. Right. Everybody ready?

EVERYONE. Yep. / Yeah. / Yes, sir. (*Etc.*)

CALLUM. I've got to get my jacket.

ANDREW. Callum, you're not coming, you're staying with the girl.

CALLUM. What? Why?

ANDREW. Cos that's an order.

JUDE. And any mistakes you know what you have to do.

CALLUM. Yes, sir.

JUDE (*quietly just to* CALLUM). I know you won't let us down, brother.

JUDE *pats* CALLUM *on the back with genuine affection. They leave.*

After agonising over it, CALLUM *finally reads* SEPHY*'s letter.*

He is in shock, shaking.

He takes a drink in to SEPHY.

SEPHY. I'm not thirsty.

CALLUM. I'll leave it here. There's a bandage, for your finger.

SEPHY *starts to wrap the bandage on her finger.* CALLUM *stays watching for a bit, about to say something, then turns to go.*

SEPHY. They've gone then?

CALLUM. Yeah.

SEPHY. I'm quite flattered that one of me could be worth five whole LM members. I guess that's the value system us Crosses have set out, so in a way, you're playing by our rules, even when you're breaking them all.

CALLUM. You should drink something.

SEPHY *picks up the bottle and regards it, smiles at*
CALLUM *and he half-smiles back. Then her whole face*
changes and she throws it at the wall.

SEPHY. What's the point when you're going to kill me?!

CALLUM. Sephy, what are you doing?

SEPHY. None of you are wearing masks, I could identify you
all. Even if Father does everything you lot want, I'm still
going to die.

CALLUM. That's not the deal.

SEPHY. Callum, don't be so naive.

CALLUM. We're setting the terms of the deal and we'll keep
them. We'll show you how we treat power with respect.

SEPHY. How can something be respectful when it's been
gained like this?

CALLUM. So Crosses gained their power respectfully, did
they? With tea and cake and no bloodshed?

SEPHY. That's not what I'm saying. I know it was obtained in
ways that should make every Cross ashamed. But that does
not mean condoning actions of equivalent violence,
aggression and evil from Noughts, this won't solve anything!

CALLUM. So you've read a couple of books now, have you?

SEPHY. I... have learnt a lot at boarding school. While you've
been training to be this... soldier, I've been training myself
too, you know, retraining, rather. Looking at things clearly,
for the first time. Truly seeing how things have been set up
by us to favour us and we have used every awful thing
available to keep it this way. We have the riches, the control
of resources, the opportunities, the land, the property and
then it all perpetuates because we keep the status quo going
and how can anyone compete?

CALLUM. Three years is a long time to be reading. What have
you actually done?

SEPHY. That is what I've done. That is my action. Learning. I have to learn before I can act otherwise my actions will be wrong. I plan to dedicate my career to finding peaceful solutions to all this…

CALLUM. There's no peaceful solution except for segregation to end.

SEPHY. I got hold of books from other places where people live equally, everything shared and each individual doing whatever it is that they're skilled in, with skin colour playing no part whatsoever – imagine! We can build this, we can build it for the future, but we have to do it together –

CALLUM. Noughts have been trying to work peacefully with Crosses – Crosses like your dad, Sephy – for decades. It doesn't work. Nothing changes. And have you ever really tried – I mean really tried – to influence your father to change things?

SEPHY. There are other ways to make change: I've hosted panels, organised conferences, sit-ins and protests –

CALLUM. Crosses aren't going to give up all those years of privilege and status with a little conference and a couple of panel talks. Always a kid. Keep your bloody sit-ins, Sephy, and I'll keep my way. This is the only thing they'll truly see and hear, this.

SEPHY. Fine. Let's not talk again until you have to end my life in, oh I guess around ten hours' time. I hope it's you that kills me. I'll beg for it to be you, to stare in your eyes as you do –

CALLUM. Stop!

SEPHY. Why? You don't care, you never did.

CALLUM. I did. I… I do.

SEPHY. Then let me go. I'd never say I saw you.

CALLUM. No. I can't, Sephy. Even if I wanted to.

SEPHY. Do you at least? Want to?

CALLUM. I have to be what I have to be, Sephy, not who I was or who I might want to be.

SEPHY. That doesn't even make sense.

CALLUM. Sephy.

SEPHY. What, Callum?

Beat. CALLUM *is not sure he should do this. He brings out the letter.*

CALLUM. Did you mean this, when you wrote it?

SEPHY. You couldn't be bothered to answer it, but you managed to keep it? You're unbelievable.

CALLUM. I... I just got it. Mum never saw me, till now, she kept it.
Sephy, were you really prepared to go away with me? To risk all that? You felt all that... for me?

Beat. All the air is sucked out of her world. He never knew.

SEPHY. I... was a fool. A little kid, like you said.

SEPHY *is upset.*

Please go, Callum.

CALLUM. Let me see your finger.

He takes her hand and it's like a switch going on, they are completely magnetised by each other.

SEPHY. Are you a doctor now as well as a freedom fighter?

Beat.

It hurts –

CALLUM *unwraps her clumsy bandaging and does an expert, gentle job. He is so tender and they get closer and closer until their noses are almost touching.* CALLUM *is finishing the bandaging as he says without looking up –*

CALLUM. Sephy, I would have gone with you.

SEPHY. What?

He looks her in the eyes, holds her face.

CALLUM. I was too scared to ever say it before, but I thought it, all the time. I love you, Sephy, I always did.

SEPHY. Callum, this is crazy –

CALLUM. Did you think about me, all this time?

SEPHY. I pushed it away, I thought you cut me off for good –

CALLUM. I thought you went away to get away from me – so I cut everything and everyone off. Or, I thought I did.

Beat.

They kiss. If movement can do the talking then great – the below text can be used as a starting point.

The way your lips kiss my skin –

SEPHY. The way your hands touch my skin –

CALLUM. Kiss.

SEPHY. Touch.

CALLUM. Fire.

SEPHY. Kiss.

CALLUM. Touch.

SEPHY. Fire.

CALLUM. Forever.

SEPHY. And ever.

A final kiss and the dance/movement stops.

CALLUM *is back to reality, looking devastated and moving away from* SEPHY. SEPHY *takes a look at him and starts to sob, adjusting her clothing and he goes to hug her but she pushes him away at the exact same time that* JUDE *pushes open the door –*

JUDE. What the hell is going on? Callum? Why is she crying? Why are her clothes all messed up? Hey?

CALLUM. She... um, I... we –

JUDE. Callum, you absolute prick!

JUDE *gets hold of* CALLUM.

Rape is gonna mean a death warrant for every LM cell in the country.

JUDE *hits* CALLUM. CALLUM *launches back at* JUDE *with fury. In the commotion,* SEPHY *steps forward and has escaped.*

Shit!

JUDE *and* CALLUM *chasing after* SEPHY *(with a gun) – they've lost her.*

JUDE. Do you know the shit we are in, ay, now?!

CALLUM. Where are the others?

JUDE. Morgan was shot. And I think they got Andrew too. Undercovers knew exactly where we'd do the drop. Someone must have told them. If we don't find her – now you've done this to her as well? You know we've got to shoot her on sight. On sight, Callum!

CALLUM. Understood.

They go different directions.

SEPHY *is on her own.*

SEPHY. I ran and I ran even though it was pitch black
    and the branches of the forest cut me
    but I couldn't feel the sting,
    I could just feel air in my face and I knew the sea wasn't far,
    the salt stuck to my lips and flipped into my eyes,
    and in that unexpected moment of aliveness I knew

that man telling Callum to get something of mine to send to
Father
I knew I'd heard his voice before
and then I couldn't place it
but now, running for my life
I remembered that word my father said in the kitchen
the word I said once too, and I knew,
the man in charge of Callum, it was the man
my father was talking to, his informant.
I kept running and I didn't scream,
tried not to breathe even,
to be as invisible as the leaves I could feel under my feet
and then –

CALLUM appears and puts his hand over SEPHY's mouth.

CALLUM. It's me. Shh. Follow the line of the trees to the left
at the clearing, you'll make it out.

SEPHY. Callum, I remember where I knew that voice, that man
who told you to get something of mine – he knows my
father, he works for him, tells him everything about the LM!

CALLUM. Sephy... thank you. One day we'll...

Noises nearby.

Just run, Sephy, run.

She runs and he shouts in the opposite direction.

The HADLEYS *are speaking on camera, and* JUDE *and*
CALLUM *can hear.*

KAMAL. I will make a short statement. My daughter is still
unconscious after being found this morning. Her doctors
describe her condition as critical but stable. Acting on
information received, we captured one of the kidnappers and
are pursuing leads to find the others. No ransom was paid.
That's all I'd like to say at this moment.

JUDE (*to* CALLUM). It never occurred to you that she could be
lying about him?

CALLUM. She wasn't.

JUDE. How can you be sure?

CALLUM. I know her! Someone betrayed us. It has to be
    Andrew.

JUDE. They'll never stop looking for us.

CALLUM. We've got to split up. Not be in any contact. Hide
    away from everything.

JUDE. That girl and her family have ruined our lives.

CALLUM. Jude, take care of yourself.

JUDE. Who knows when we'll see each other again, bro – but
    let me give you some free advice. Stay away from
    Persephone Hadley. Or she's going to be the death of you.

JASMINE. Thank God she's alive. We are so thankful.

MINERVA. We are so thankful.

SEPHY. And that was what I was supposed to do too.
    Thank God. Be thankful. Smile, but sadly.
    Say no word against my father's speeches of disdain
    laden with insane promises of retribution
    to the Liberation Militia who had 'abused' me.
    I was not to speak my thoughts
    on how I blamed my father,
    our most likely next Prime Minister,
    for his own regressive feelings allowing
    such sinister furies to gather and gain acclaim.
    And the main thing of course,
    I must never ever say
    never ever admit
    never ever
    that I agree with their aim,
    if not with their actions.
    And of course,
    I can never ever ever ever

ever ever admit
that – me and Callum did it!
I can't believe it, my first time
and it was –
weird, since I was kidnapped, obviously.
But also, somehow, perfect.
And I laugh to myself
about how I'd make it better next time
and then one day I'm like,
why do I feel so sick?
And Minerva is like –

MINERVA (*giving her a pregnancy test*). Sephy, we'll get through this together, okay?

SEPHY. Okay. Okay.

She goes for a pee.

MINERVA. How can you be so calm?

SEPHY. What do you mean?

MINERVA. When… they raped you?

SEPHY. No, Minnie – it wasn't –

MINERVA. I'm so sorry, Sephy.

SEPHY. But it wasn't –

MINERVA *has the test by this point.*

MINERVA. Oh God – (*Showing* SEPHY.) I'm sorry, Sephy –

SEPHY. Lines.

MINERVA. Blue –

SEPHY. Two –

MINERVA. Blue –

SEPHY. Lines.

MINERVA. You're –

SEPHY. I'm –

MINERVA. My God, those monsters!

SEPHY. But, Minnie –

MINERVA *rushes around.*

MINERVA. Okay, stay calm.
Seph, there's a place we can go, a clinic we can pay, today.
Unless – maybe you want to tell the police so there's another
charge in the case – is that what you want? And then we can
delay the clinic but it would mean telling Mum and Dad…
Sephy, maybe you should tell Mum and Dad. Maybe they
should know…

SEPHY. Wait. Just. I need. A minute.

MINERVA. Look. I know we haven't always been close, Sephy,
but with this, you can trust me, I swear to you, you're my
little sister and… how could they do this!

SEPHY. I wasn't raped, Minnie.

MINERVA. What do you mean?

SEPHY. I want to have this baby.

MINERVA. You've been through so much.

SEPHY. Don't touch me. I know what I want. I want the baby.
Please, Minerva, don't tell Mum and Dad…

SEPHY *starts rubbing her stomach.* MINERVA *starts
calling on her phone.*

CALLUM. Left now,
on the run
on my own.
The only way it can be,
lonely.
Weeks since I saw a face I know who knows me.
Disguised, hiding, stranger.
Want to see Sephy so badly,

I pass TV shops to see her picture on the news,
'hunt for her captors still on'
written huge across that face,
that face that feels like home.
Until one day, what they say changes.
My hand up at the window,
my jaw on the floor.
Can it be true?
She's really having –

SEPHY. A baby. I never wanted a baby.
    I always said, if I ever got pregnant by accident,
    I'd have an abortion.
    So confident, so clear.
    Who wanted a baby to bring down all those years
    of striving to build myself up?
    I knew from my own mother how tough
    it was to build a self and another.
    But this was me and Callum.
    And it was more than that even.
    I could feel its power even as I was heaving
    over the toilet every morning,
    even as my ankles swelled
    I felt its light lift all my weight
    and after Minnie told them, everyone gathered round –
    Mother Father Sister
    doctors lawyers counsellors
    everyone saying the same thing –

JASMINE. You've been through a lot, Persephone –

MINERVA. It's not the right time, Sephy –

KAMAL. You're not in the right state of mind, Persephone –

JASMINE. You're far too young, Sephy, your life has just
    begun, Sephy –

SEPHY. The papers talk of PTSD,
    the TV hosts ask every guest

'What do you make of Persephone Hadley
keeping the baby of rapists?'
And I say again and again and again –
I was not raped. But Minnie won't let it go –

MINERVA. Sephy, did you know the man who did this, from
    before?
    Sephy, tell me.

SEPHY. But I never ever say his name except on my own,
    when I talk to the baby and tell it stories of us
    on the beach or at school or as kids in the sea.

MINERVA. Sephy, did Callum McGregor do this?

SEPHY. And I deny and deny but my face can't lie
    And then his face, my Callum's face,
    is all over the screens –
    Cos Minnie betrayed me.
    Most wanted, it says – most wanted,
    reward, reward, reward,
    and I realise I can never see him again.
    But then.
    Whistle on my window. I know.
    Down to the rose garden, I go.

CALLUM. Sephy.

SEPHY. Callum, it's not safe here. How did you even get in?

CALLUM. I had to see you. Is it – is it true?

SEPHY. Yes.

CALLUM. Sephy, this is… just amazing.

SEPHY. If it's a boy I'll call him Ryan.

CALLUM. And if it's a girl – Rose. After this garden.

SEPHY. Callie Rose!

CALLUM. That's terrible!

SEPHY. It's perfect.

Beat.

CALLUM. Sephy –
Let's get out of here, now. I've saved some money. We can get a boat away from here. Is it worth the risk? You, me, the baby –

SEPHY. Yes, yes –

GUARDS. FREEZE!

SEPHY. Callum, run!

GUARDS *grab* CALLUM, *and* SEPHY *screams.*

KAMAL *and a heavily pregnant* SEPHY *are circling each other.*

KAMAL. Sephy, just say it.

SEPHY. I won't.

KAMAL. He'll live if you do.

SEPHY. He'd never be alive again if I did.

KAMAL. Sephy – he raped you!

SEPHY. We *made love*, Dad – how's that? We made love and now your grandchild is going to pop out half Nought and –

KAMAL. Stop it. You've lost your mind. You leave me no choice.

SEPHY. And you leave me none either.

As they separate, KAMAL *goes one way and* SEPHY *the other.*

I've never made a public statement before, but I've been left with no choice, having been stopped from giving evidence at a trial about the alleged crime against me. So I want the

whole world to know, Callum McGregor did not rape me and
I am *thrilled* to soon be having our baby –

KAMAL *goes to* CALLUM *in his cell.*

KAMAL. You can save yourself, Callum, and I'll ensure you
will be out of prison in no more than eight years. You'll still
have your whole life ahead of you.

CALLUM. I have no life without Sephy and the baby.

KAMAL. You realise she's only having the baby because she
feels guilty? You're going to die! How can she not keep your
baby? If you sign this to say the charges against you are true,
then you won't die. Watch how, as soon as she knows you'll
live, she'll give the baby away.

CALLUM. Did she tell you that?

KAMAL. Of course. She'll give the baby up at birth.

CALLUM. I don't believe you. I've heard the news. Sephy
announcing that she's thrilled to be having our baby, that the
charges against me are false.

KAMAL. She can't let you hear her say anything else. But it is
what she wants you to do. Don't you think she'd have found
a way to come here and see you otherwise?

He hits a nerve with CALLUM, *who is unsure of the truth now.*

CALLUM. Die and my baby stays with its loving mother or
live and my baby gets sent away –

KAMAL. It will be looked after very well and –

CALLUM. That's the choice you're giving me? How can you
make sense of this in your head? What difference would it
make to your life if me and Sephy went off to live together
somewhere far away? You've never even cared about her
anyway, so is it more that a Cross and a Nought having a
baby together shakes the foundations of your whole world so
/ much that – ?

KAMAL. Enough! Just sign the paper, boy.

CALLUM *takes the paper, looks at* KAMAL, *rips it up*.

CALLUM. Guard! Please see Mr Hadley out.

KAMAL. Your child will not be welcome here, you know that, don't you, Callum? You're ruining two lives – the child's and Persephone's – by ending your own. I knew Noughts were stupid, but if that's what you want then so be it.

CALLUM. What time is it, Jackie?

JACKIE. Ten to six.

CALLUM. Ten minutes. That's still long enough for a reprieve.

JACKIE. If you say so, son.

CALLUM. You said the papers all questioned the death sentence in my case. The grounds are not strong enough.

JACKIE. There's no harm in hoping. And look what happened with your dad.

CALLUM. Exactly.

CALLUM *has a pack of cards*.

Will you play?

JACKIE. Sure.

CALLUM *(as he deals)*. Do you ever wonder what it would be like if our situations were reversed? If we Noughts were in charge instead of you Crosses?

JACKIE. I don't really see us as being in charge, you know, my life isn't exactly a walk in the park.

CALLUM. Tomorrow, though, you will be able to walk in the park, won't you?

JACKIE. Fair point.

CALLUM. I used to think about it a lot. A world with no more discrimination, no more prejudice – 'a level playing field'.

JACKIE. Sounds like a fairy tale, Callum. If you ask me, people are people. Power corrupts. Doesn't matter the colour of your skin.

CALLUM. No. If there was no oppression of any one group, everything would be different. We would share power. Power wouldn't even be power the way we think of it, without oppression. Decisions would be taken after thinking about the impact they'd have on the most amount of people. We would be accountable. We would give our lives for everyone to keep being treated the same. We can change what power means, Jackie. You have to believe that – I do.

Beat. Card put down.

JACKIE. You're a brave young man.

Beat.

You know, Persephone Hadley. She did try to get in here to see you – more than once as well. And your mum. Did everything they could to get a minute with you. But orders were from the top – no visitors, no matter what.

CALLUM *nods.*

It's time. You're doing fine. Be strong.

On the side where MEGGIE *and* CALLUM *sat during* RYAN's *execution, a very pregnant* SEPHY *now sits with* MEGGIE, *who holds her hand. On the side where the* HADLEYS *sat before, there is just* KAMAL *and* JASMINE, *watching.* MINERVA *is somewhere in the middle.*

CALLUM *is led by a* GUARD, *he is searching for* SEPHY. *The clock chimes. One, he sees her, their eyes meet. Two, the hood is pulled over his head and, three,* SEPHY *shouts:*

SEPHY. I love you, Callum!

Four, SEPHY *shouts again –*

And our child will love you!

Five, CALLUM *shouts but the hood is muffling the sound –*

CALLUM. I love you too!

Six, CALLUM *is executed.*

SEPHY *screams and screams and this transforms itself into her having the baby – through soundscape and music. By the end she is on an empty stage on her own holding Callie Rose.*

Epilogue

SEPHY. When a newborn baby cries
it means there's life
and with new life there's new hope,
right?

The End.

GREAT EXPECTATIONS
Nick Ormerod and Declan Donnellan
Adapted from Charles Dickens

THE HAUNTING
Hugh Janes
Adapted from Charles Dickens

HIS DARK MATERIALS
Nicholas Wright
Adapted from Philip Pullman

THE HOUND OF THE BASKERVILLES
Steven Canny & John Nicholson
Adapted from Arthur Conan Doyle

JANE EYRE
Polly Teale
Adapted from Charlotte Brontë

JEEVES AND WOOSTER IN PERFECT NONSENSE
The Goodale Brothers
Adapted from P.G. Wodehouse

THE JUNGLE BOOK
Jessica Swale and Joe Stilgoe
Adapted from Rudyard Kipling

KENSUKE'S KINGDOM
Stuart Paterson
Adapted from Michael Morpurgo

KES
Lawrence Till
Adapted from Barry Hines

MARY SHELLEY'S FRANKENSTEIN
Rona Munro
Adapted from Mary Shelley

THE MASSIVE TRAGEDY OF MADAME BOVARY
John Nicholson & Javier Marzan
Adapted from Gustave Flaubert

NORTHANGER ABBEY
Tim Luscombe
Adapted from Jane Austen

PERSUASION
Mark Healy
Adapted from Jane Austen

PRIDE AND PREJUDICE (SORT OF)
Isobel McArthur
After Jane Austen

THE RAGGED TROUSERED PHILANTHROPISTS
Howard Brenton
Adapted from Robert Tressell

THE RAILWAY CHILDREN
Mike Kenny
Adapted from E. Nesbit

SENSE AND SENSIBILITY
Mark Healy
Adapted from Jane Austen

SWALLOWS AND AMAZONS
Helen Edmundson and Neil Hannon
Adapted from Arthur Ransome

THE THREE MUSKETEERS
John Nicholson & Le Navet Bete
Adapted from Alexander Dumas

TREASURE ISLAND
Stuart Paterson
Adapted from Robert Louis Stevenson

THE WIND IN THE WILLOWS
Mike Kenny
Adapted from Kenneth Grahame

WUTHERING HEIGHTS
Andrew Sheridan
Adapted from Emily Brontë

www.nickhernbooks.co.uk

facebook.com/nickhernbooks

twitter.com/nickhernbooks